S0-BLY-624

The Fastest Way to Create a Memorable

SPEECH

ASAP

by
William Mooney & Donald J. Noone Ph.D.

BARRON'S

DEDICATION

To our wives, Valorie Goodall Mooney and Rosemarie Noone,
who have always encouraged us to do what makes us happy and
who gave us positive inspiration all along the way.

© Copyright 1992 by William Mooney and Donald J. Noone

All rights reserved.

No part of this book may be reproduced in any form, by photostat,
microfilm, xerography, or any other means, or incorporated into any
information retrieval system, electronic or mechanical, without the
written permission of the copyright owner.

All inquiries should be addressed to:
Barron's Educational Series, Inc.
250 Wireless Boulevard
Hauppauge, New York 11788

Library of Congress Catalog Card No.: 92-2794

International Standard Book No. 0-8120-6280-9

Library of Congress Cataloging-in-Publication Data

Mooney, William.
    ASAP : the fastest way to create a memorable speech / William
Mooney & Donald Noone.
      p.   cm.

    ISBN 0-8120-6280-9
    I. Noone, Donald J. II. Title.
PN4121.M586 1992
808.5'1 — dc20
                                     92-2794
                                     CIP

PRINTED IN THE UNITED STATES OF AMERICA

2345   6550   987654321

Table of Contents

List of Figures

Introduction

WHY ASAP?

ASAP is designed specifically for anyone who has to give a speech and is pressed for time — anyone who needs to come up with a memorable speech as soon as possible. It is for anyone who has ever had a hard time putting together an effective speech. It is for anyone — a businessperson, student, engineer, housewife, preacher, first-time speaker, or skilled orator.

Speed, along with quality, is our overriding concern. Therefore, instead of giving you a number of different ways to assemble a speech, we offer *one* easy time-crunching method that will serve you effectively in most speaking situations. We all have busy schedules these days; but even when we are given a month to prepare a speech, many of us put it off until the last minute. Panic sets in, and what could have been an exciting opportunity rapidly becomes a painful ordeal.

With the ASAP method, you need never worry again about fast-approaching deadlines. You can create a terrific speech regardless of the time you have to prepare it. ASAP is unique — even revolutionary.

WHAT'S SO SPECIAL ABOUT ASAP?

We have spent a lot of time working with businesspeople — middle managers to high-level executives — to help them overcome their problems with public speaking. From these sessions, we observed the businesspeople had a number of common traits: they were under tremendous time pressures; they did not know how to put together an effective speech; they did not know what makes a speech memorable; they were reluctant to display any enthusiasm; and they did not fully appreciate how important good presentations can be to their future careers. Yet they were all looking for a fast, easy way to create a good speech.

We read most of the books on public speaking and found that, although there is a lot of good information contained in each one, there is no *fast* guide that is *effective* for creating a *memorable* speech. Fast, effective, and memorable, then, became our three watchwords.

We started asking ourselves what kind of book would we like to read that could give us the speed and technique to create a memorable speech every time. Since we're both inveterate procrastinators, we understand all too well the pressure of a time crunch. We also understand the desperation that comes from having to produce a speech when you don't know what you're doing. With that in mind, we started trying out various methods that would be effective in most speaking situations.

Our goal was to come up with a method that is easy and fast to learn, and at the same time one that would give you, the speaker, a solid structure from which to create a memorable speech fast. We believe the ASAP method meets that goal.

HOW LONG DOES IT TAKE TO PUT TOGETHER AN ASAP SPEECH?
How Much Time Do You Have?

Once you master the ASAP method (a very easy trick), you will find it is so effective you can actually prepare your speech on the way to the podium!

In fact, if you are really in a rush right now and have to give a talk in half an hour, skip directly to Chapter 13 and learn "How to Prepare Your Speech on the Way to the Podium." Chapter 13 provides you with the answer to your prayers. If your speaking situation is not on red alert, however, the first time you work through the ASAP format will take a little longer.

How Much Longer?

Give yourself at least a couple of hours to construct a creditable speech. Even so, as any speechmaker knows, that is really fast. We have structured this book so that you work along with us. If you follow our instructions, you will have created a memorable speech by the time you finish Chapter 9.

How?

We show you how to use time-proven memory aids that enable both you and your audience to remember the speech. We spell out the importance of using a prop to create and illustrate your speech and make it memorable. We show you how to use mind maps to dump all your thoughts and ideas onto one page. Then we give you specific guidelines on how to bring order out of the chaos of your original thoughts; and we give you models to imitate. It is a simple format that is free from jargon and abstraction. And as we said, once you learn the ASAP method and its basic components, you can literally prepare your speech on the way to the podium (see Chapter 13).

WHAT ARE THE PAYOFFS FOR YOU?

You will feel good about the experience, you will increase your chances of moving your audience, and your personal reputation and even your business career can be improved.

In business, for example, most enlightened managers hold frequent meetings that require employees to speak often and on a variety of issues. These managers are always judging their staff, always asking themselves, "Does this employee have a future? Is this person one of my leading lights?" Employees are always judged by how well they speak. Every time you get up to speak, it becomes "performance evaluation time." Your career is literally on the line. If you speak well, you will find yourself on the fast track within your organization. If you speak poorly, your career can sink like a stone in the water. Peter Drucker, the noted management consultant, wrote in *Fortune* magazine that the one basic skill that is most valuable for any employee is "the ability to organize and express ideas in writing and speaking." ASAP teaches you that skill.

Speaking opportunities occur everywhere: schools, churches, and civic events, for example. Think back to the times when you were in the audience listening to someone speak. What judgments did you make about the speech or the speaker — about what was said and the way it was said? Remember your feelings when the speaker was bad? Keep in mind that people will be making the same judgments about you — judgments about your words, your appearance, your ideas, your presentation. This is not meant to frighten you, but to make you aware of how much is at stake when you speak before a group.

With this book, we are saying don't worry about that anymore. Follow our method and you will excel. We show you how to organize and present your thoughts. We take away most of your pre-speech anxiety by giving you a method that is quick, effective, and memorable.

The ASAP method not only evaporates time constraints, but it gives you the flexibility to edit your speech on the spot. Let's say you are scheduled to give a twenty-minute talk, but because previous speakers exceeded their time allotment, the coordinator informs you that your time has been cut to six minutes. Most speakers would be thrown into a panic by this. When you use ASAP's outline of key words and phrases, you can easily pare down your talk and still be effective.

When you follow our by-the-numbers approach and answer each question completely, you will discover that the ASAP method creates a logical, coherent, interesting, effective, and memorable speech every time — a speech that gets results. In short, the ASAP method helps you to be a star when the limelight hits you. Give it a try. You will soon discover it is the only method you will ever need.

1

What Is the ASAP Method?

ASAP stands for *as soon as possible.* ASAP is simply the fastest, most direct way you can create a speech from scratch.

ASAP'S FEATURES

1. A *question and answer* format.
2. *Examples* to be studied and imitated.
3. A *prop* — only one audiovisual aid.
4. *Mind maps* — which speed creativity.
5. *Analogy, parallels,* and *association* — which supply inspiration and structure while ensuring retention of your message by both you and your listeners.
6. An *outline* format — the speech is not written out.
7. *The ASAP shell* (key words and phrases) — adaptable to any talk.
8. *One* powerful way to end the talk.

WHAT IS THE METHOD?

ASAP means more than *as soon as possible:*

A stands for: *Ask* — the right questions.
S stands for: *Study* — the answers and examples.
A stands for: *Adapt* — the information to your situation.
P stands for: *Produce* — a quality speech.

Ask the Right Questions

The best way to solve a problem is to know what questions to ask, that is, the right questions. Questions focus our attention, direct our thinking, and provoke responses. The right questions make the hunt for the right answers easier. We supply a series of right questions that lead you through the ASAP method. Once you answer them, you are well on your way to creating a quality speech.

Study the Answers and Examples

In addition to finding the right answers to the right questions, the quickest way to learn something is to imitate good examples. Language, dance, and ski instructors, among others, have long used imitation as an effective method of teaching. When you were an infant, you learned to talk by imitating the sounds your family made. In the business world, Panasonic built an enormous company based purely upon imitation and improvement. ASAP gives you many examples to study, imitate, and improve upon.

Adapt the Information to Your Situation

Not only does ASAP provide you with the right questions and excellent examples, but it shows you how to apply the information to your present speech opportunity. We introduce you to the magic of a prop. Then we show you how to use your prop to assemble and organize your speech, simply and coherently, through the techniques of analogy and transfer.

Produce a Quality Speech that Gets Results

That is what ASAP is really all about — results. What results do we want you to achieve?

1. *A memorable speech* — a speech that the audience will remember, and you will too.
2. *An effective speech* — a speech that accomplishes your intended result.
3. *A respectable speech* — a speech you are proud of.
4. *A self-confident speech* — a speech filled with good material, one that allows you to reach out and grab the audience's attention and hold it to the end.
5. *A coherent speech* — a speech that flows logically from the beginning through the middle to the end.

STEPS TO TAKE

We know there are 123 other ways to create a speech. We give you just *one* way — a way that gets results.

The ASAP speech has four parts:

1. BEGINNING
    A. Introduction of your prop. A prop gets the audience's attention, one of the most difficult problems any speaker faces.
    B. An orderly presentation of the pluses and minuses associated with your prop.
2. BRIDGE
    A. A simple statement of the relationship between your *prop* and the *subject of comparison,* employing a question, an answer, an analogy, and the order of your *persuasion points.*
    B. "Tells them what you're going to tell them."
3. MIDDLE
    A. An orderly elaboration of the persuasion points associated with your *subject of comparison* and

intended result, with frequent references to your
prop points.
B.   "Tells them."
4.   ENDING
A.   A summary of the major persuasion points
couched in terms of the pain to be avoided and
the rewards to be reaped.
B.   "Tells them what you told them."
C.   A call for action. (Your *intended result*.)
"Tells them *what you want them to do.*"
D.   Final linkage — *Prop* to *subject of comparison.*

We believe imitation is the fastest way to learn anything;
therefore, we provide you with a number of examples that
illustrate each aspect of the ASAP method. We have chosen our
examples from business, politics, and education. Some of them
may directly parallel your own speaking situation. But regardless of your particular challenge, we urge you to study our
examples carefully. They will give you greater insight into the
ASAP process and will undoubtedly shed light on aspects of
your particular problem.

Along with our many diverse examples, we have included an
ongoing example that we develop in greater detail. We follow the
story of Joe Parent, showing you the results of his decisions each
step of the way, from his initial decision to speak to the day he
delivers his speech before the assembled school board.

Joe Parent serves as a kind of "Everyman" (or, to be politically
correct, "Everyperson") in a speaking situation.

- He has a cause.
- He is involved in a conflict situation.
- He has strong opponents.
- He needs to persuade them that his cause is right.
- He has very little time to prepare his speech.
- He has even less time to deliver it.

Joe Parent's situation is not a worst-case scenario, but it is
certainly a challenging one. Since most of you will have more

favorable circumstances than Joe Parent in which to assemble your speech, your job using the ASAP method will be much easier.

Joe Parent's story is rooted in fact. It stems from an actual community conflict. We simply changed the names to protect those who might not be presented in a favorable light.

ONGOING EXAMPLE

The problems faced when teachers, parents, and the school board collide are common to most of us. So we have chosen this type of dramatic meeting as our ongoing example. Most of us either attended public schools or have children who attend them. If not, we have certainly heard or read about these public school conflicts. Invariably, they are tense and confrontational — difficult situations in which to give a speech. We have included an extensive background scenario for Joe Parent's speech, because we think the lessons drawn from his example are applicable across a broad spectrum of speaking situations. Therefore, we urge you to carefully study the background and examples because they can save you a lot of time in your preparation.

Background to the Ongoing Example (Joe Parent's Story)

School Superintendent Gold retired after devoting twenty-three years to making Jefferson one of the top-rated school districts in the state. Mr. Gold was replaced by Mr. Brons who, toward the end of his first year in office, convinced the school board to adopt his plan to give Jefferson an even greater reputation for quality education.

The heart of Superintendent Brons's plan contained a proposal to create "magnet" schools on the elementary level — one school to attract students skilled in the arts, another for science, another for higher mathematics, and so on.

The new magnet school plan would require new administrators

specialized in those areas. It would also call for the addition of curriculum supervisors and assistant superintendents. In addition to the magnet schools, Superintendent Brons proposed a drug prevention program (costing $400,000), a self-esteem program for students (costing $300,000), and an in-service training program for teachers (costing $200,000). The drug/alcohol and self-esteem programs would demand expensive outside consultants.

At roughly the same time the Jefferson school board approved Mr. Brons's proposal, the Jefferson teachers' contract expired. Their union was demanding a seven percent per year increase on a new two-year contract.

It didn't take long for the ax to fall. Fifty-nine tenured and untenured teachers received notices that they would not be rehired. The notices simply stated there was to be a Reduction In Force (RIF). The teachers' union protested the RIF notices, but the school board remained firm. It supported Superintendent Brons's plan to make the township's schools even more distinguished. However, because there was not enough money in the budget to institute the new programs *and* cover the cost of a new teacher's contract, the board reasoned that dismissing fifty-nine teachers would solve its fiscal problems.

Joe Parent had moved his family to Jefferson because of its reputation for having a superior school system. Joe felt that the teachers' dismissal was uncalled for, that they should be rehired immediately. He called the school board and demanded to be heard. Joe was told the board had scheduled a special meeting for tomorrow night and that he could be one of ten speakers from the community.

Now that you have read the background for the ongoing example and understand Joe's dilemma, we will explain his choices each step of the way and show you how he creates a strong, effective speech.

2

Start at the End

Let's begin!

THE ASAP PROCESS

A — Ask yourself the right questions.
S — Study the answers and examples we provide.
A— Adapt our answers and examples to your situation.
P— Produce a quality speech by answering each question.

The ASAP method is interactive. You work along with us. We ask questions that get right to the point, then answer them clearly and concisely. As you move through this simple process, we explain our rationale for each question, as well as any terms with which you may be unfamiliar. There are examples every step of the way. Follow our steps and answer each question thoroughly. When you do, you will find ASAP is indeed the fastest way to create a memorable speech.

This is your first question:

QUESTION: What *result* do I intend to bring about by giving my talk?

ANSWER: Whether you are making a formal presentation, selling a product, disseminating information, or just introducing another speaker, you want some *result* to occur. A *result* is what you intend to accomplish by giving your speech. For example, you are reading this book because you want to learn a fast, clear-cut method for persuading a group of people *to do something;* that is your intended result. You want to learn how to persuade the audience to make a change. What kind of change? Perhaps you wish to change the way they think, feel, or act.

You want to move them from point A (where they are *before* you speak) to point B (where you want them to be *after* you speak). Every *result* in speechmaking is a movement by the audience from point A to point B. Point B is your *intended result.*

Example of Intended Result		
Point A		Point B
From not buying	to	buying
From not voting	to	voting
From not supporting an issue	to	supporting an issue
From lack of knowledge	to	enlightenment

Since it is always the speaker's intention to move the audience from one point to another, it is our view that: *Every speech is a persuasive speech.* But, in order to persuade an audience to do something, you must define exactly what you want them to do. You must come up with a clear, unambiguous statement of your intended result.

Once you clearly define and state your intended result, the whole process of making an effective speech answers the question "What can I say that will motivate this audience to change and give me the result I intend?" Therefore, your first step — before you assemble your speech — is to clearly define and state your intended result.

This is the result Joe Parent desires: "I have to convince the Jefferson school board to rehire the fifty-nine teachers they dismissed." As you can see, Joe's intended result is a simple, clear statement of purpose.

YOUR INTENDED RESULT

In order to get a more specific handle on the intended result before you put your talk together, it is important for you to: Know your audience and think of them at all times. Why? Because you want the audience to do as you suggest. To accomplish this, it is necessary to know certain aspects of the speaking situation. You have to know what is important to your audience and what is not important to them. You have to get inside their skin and see the world from their point of view.

You should always ask, "What must I do to satisfy the audience's needs?" Only by satisfying them will you meet your own needs. They will never act on your suggestion unless it benefits them. Therefore, your main task is to figure out exactly how your intended result will benefit the audience.

To help you determine the benefits, we suggest you think of yourself as a high-powered investigative reporter whose job is to ferret out all you can about this speaking situation. Ask and answer the six classic journalistic questions: who, what, when, where, why, and how.

- *Why* am I giving this talk? *Why* will the audience be there?
- *Who* is in the audience?
- *What* is the audience's position?

- *When* will my talk be given?
- *Where* on the program am I?
- *How* long should I talk?

Once you answer these questions, you will be able to define your intended result with greater precision.

QUESTION: *Why* am I giving this talk?

ANSWER: Every talk is given for a reason. Therefore, it is important to know *why* you committed yourself to this speaking engagement. Did you initiate the talk? Were you invited or told to give the talk? If you do not know the answer, call the person who asked or told you to speak.

Why is Joe Parent making a speech? Joe wants to persuade the school board to rehire the fifty-nine teachers so his children's chances for a quality education will not be hurt.

Other Examples of "Why I Am Giving This Talk"

"I feel I can really help my company improve its sales and generate more net income in the process."

"I am the only person in town who knows something about toxic waste. That is why I was invited to speak."

"My boss is going on vacation. She delegated to me the task of making a presentation to the construction committee."

"I can enhance my reputation, meet new people, and make business contacts."

Apply the explanations and examples to your situation. Think about them; then produce a response that makes sense for your particular situation. The answer will help suggest your intended result.

APPLICATION: The reason I have this speaking engagement is

_____

_____

QUESTION: Why will the audience be attending?

ANSWER: As we said, there are only three reasons for making a speech:

1. You are asked to.
2. You are told to.
3. You want to.

Likewise, audiences attend speaking events for three reasons:

1. They were asked to be there.
2. They were told to be there.
3. They want to be there.

It is possible some people might be there simply to get out of the cold; their number will, we hope, be few. In any event, each reason casts a different light on the result you want to accomplish. It affects *what* you say and *how* you say it.

Joe Parent knows the community has forced the school board to hold this meeting. The board has to defend its actions. Many townspeople will attend because they are upset about the teachers' dismissal. They want to be there. Obviously the ten concerned citizens who are speaking want to be there.

Other Examples of "Why the Audience Is Here"

The audience is captive — "You must attend!"

The audience has voluntarily chosen to be there.

The audience is there simply because it is a social occasion; you are incidental.

APPLICATION: My audience will be there because _____

Once you know why both you and the audience are attending, the next step is to take a close look at the audience's composition.

QUESTION: Who will be in the audience?

ANSWER: You always want the audience to accept and act upon your intended result. Otherwise you're speaking to no avail, simply tossing words to the wind. Therefore, it makes good sense to know *who* your audience is, *what* is important to them, and *why* they think and act the way they do. You need to find out what education they have, what type of work they do, where their interests lie, what values they hold important.

Once you find out *who* will be in the audience, you are on the road to discovering what's important to them. Find out all you can about them. You never know when something useful might crop up. Constantly ask yourself: "What can I learn about this audience that, at the end of my speech, will motivate them to march right into my camp?" Of course, each audience will be different, but that is precisely why it is necessary to identify the attributes that might affect your talk.

Realize every moment you are speaking that each person in the audience is asking: "What's in it for me?" You must be able to answer that question if you are going to motivate them to change. Your guiding principle should be: "I will address what's important to them, not what's important to me." You will never persuade any audience if your proposal does not either benefit them or show them how to avoid dire consequences, either offer them rewards or the avoidance of pain; only these alternatives give your listeners plausible reasons for changing the way you want them to. Don't waste time on points that don't hit home. Uncover the attributes of your audience that are important to the result you want to make happen.

Joe Parent phoned the school and found out the general background of the school board. Joe had clearly defined his intended result. The two important questions he wanted answered were (1) How many of the board members have children in school? and (2) How many on the school board are homeowners? Joe thought that of all the attributes associated with the board, they most valued money and their children (not necessarily in that order).

APPLICATION: Who will be in the audience? (e.g., age, sex, education, cultural/religious background, the roles they play, decision makers present) _____

_____

_____

QUESTION: What position does the audience hold on my subject?

ANSWER: It is important that you answer this question as fully as possible. To be an effective persuader, you need to know not only *who* will be in the audience, but *what* positions about your subject they might have.

Find the answers to these questions:

1. What prejudices do they have about my subject?
2. How much do they already know about my subject?
3. What is their level of sophistication?
4. How open or close minded are they?

When you know what prejudices they have, you can speak directly to those prejudices. When you find out what the audience already knows about your subject, you can determine whether you must spend more or less time bringing them up to speed. The same holds true for their level of sophistication. The more knowledgeable an audience is about your subject, the less time you need to spend on background.

What an audience feels and thinks influences what you say and how you say it. Therefore, find out all you can about their positions and attitudes on your subject. It always helps to know what might stand in your way.

Joe Parent knows the Jefferson school board will be defensive about its dismissal of the fifty-nine teachers. He thinks the board will be reluctant to back down and withdraw its endorsement of the superintendent's new plans.

Other Examples of "What Position the Audience Has"

The audience is hostile about the position you represent.

Half the audience is for you, half against you.

The audience is neutral — a blank slate.

The audience is eager to hear you. (On this occasion it will be like preaching to the choir.)

Apply these considerations to your situation and come up with an answer that is responsive to the condition of your audience. Do this *now* before you take another step.

APPLICATION: The major (audience-related) factors I am up against or might have going for me are _____

_____

_____

_____

_____

QUESTION: *When* will my talk be given?

ANSWER: Anytime you attempt to persuade people, you always stand a better chance if they are not fatigued. Early morning is usually best if you have a choice. If the audience is fatigued, has just eaten, or has had a lot to drink, your job will be more difficult. (By the way, never speak to people who have had too much to drink unless you're paid a lot of money to endure their abuse.)

Joe Parent found out the school board meeting starts at 7 p.m. The concerned citizens, like Joe, will be heard starting at 8:30 p.m. Joe knows he has to do something to stand out and get the school board's attention because their energy level will surely be flagging.

Other Examples of "When My Talk Will Be Given"

It's evening. The audience has enjoyed an extended happy hour. Two bottles of wine are on each dinner table.

It's right after lunch and everyone is drowsy.

It's 4:45 p.m. People are at the low end of their biorhythmic scale. They are also thinking about heading for home.

It's early morning. Everyone is fresh and energetic.

APPLICATION: My speech is scheduled for _____ and this is important because _____

QUESTION: *Where* on the program am I?

ANSWER: If you are tenth in a long list of speakers, that position alone will dictate what you say, how you say it, and how long you take to say it. Chances are, people in the audience will be praying that you only say two or three sentences and sit down. Perhaps there has been a long meeting just before your presentation. All these variables will affect what you say and how long you take to say it.

Joe Parent is the seventh of ten speakers. Joe knows he must do something unique to stand out from the rest of the speakers and capture the board's attention. He also knows he must be brief and get to the point quickly.

APPLICATION: I am the _____ [first, second] _____ speaker out of _____ [ten, fifteen] _____ speakers. My position is in the _____ [first quarter, second quarter] _____ of the program. This is important because _____

_____

_____

QUESTION: *How long* should I talk?

ANSWER: If you have been invited, ask your sponsor how long the speech should be. In the absence of a guideline, we suggest anything up to twenty minutes as the best length. In any case, never exceed fifty minutes. Audiences are always grateful if the talk is short. As Mark Twain said, "It's a terrible death to be talked to death." The amount of material you use and its complexity are directly influenced by how long you speak.

Joe Parent was told he would be allotted six minutes to present his argument. He was also told the time limit would be strictly enforced.

APPLICATION: My talk will be _____ minutes long. This is important because _____

_____

QUESTION: In what way does this analysis of the speaking situation alter my *intended result?*

ANSWER: This brings us back full circle to the result you wish to accomplish. Now that you have answered all the questions above, it's time to formulate with crystal clarity the result you intend to accomplish. The audience analysis you have just completed may have altered the result you originally proposed.

If so, change your result to fit your analysis. Remember: State your intended result in *one* simple declarative sentence.

Joe Parent still wants the fifty-nine teachers rehired immediately.

APPLICATION: The result I want to accomplish is _____

_____

_____

_____

_____

How to persuade the audience to accept your proposal is the problem you will solve with the rest of our questions. The next important segment of the ASAP method is "Select a Prop."

3

Select a Prop

A prop is any object you display during your talk. We use the word *prop* in the theatrical sense; it is short for *property*. Theatrical properties are objects that actors handle on stage, such as teacups, letters, books, telephones, fans, walking sticks, spectacles, cigarette holders, handbags, vases, or lamps.

The use of a prop is at the core of the ASAP method. It is a brand new way to prepare and deliver a speech. Once you learn our method, you will appreciate the advantage it has over other approaches. There are five reasons why a prop is such a powerful tool for speechmaking:

1. A prop immediately captures your audience's curiosity and attention.
2. A prop solves your audiovisual problems — you display only one object.
3. A prop frames your talk and provides inspiration for your persuasion points.
4. A prop provides vivid, tangible hooks for your persuasion points, enabling you to anchor the talk not only in your memory, but in the memory of the audience as well.
5. A prop dramatically reduces your preparation time.

Each one of these reasons is consistent with the latest research on memory and creativity.

QUESTION: What prop should I use?

ANSWER: Anything.

Take a look around you. Pick up something within your reach: a pencil, a calculator, a hammer, a deer head with antlers, an eggbeater, a glass, a telephone...anything.

However, although you can use anything as a prop, there is a big difference between theatrical props and the prop we want you to choose. Theater props are used in context with the business of a play. They are plausible. The prop we want you to choose is *not* used in context with your subject. It should be implausible, out of context from its usual surroundings. Theater props are unobtrusive, playing only minor roles. Our prop says, "Look at me! I'm a great big bizarre star!"

The Criteria for a Good Prop

- It's implausible.
- It's out of context from its usual surroundings.
- It's *not* connected with the result you want.
- It arouses curiosity.
- It's surprising.
- It could even be weird, strange, or bizarre.

As illogical as it may seem, the more of these qualities your prop has, the more effective it will be.

For example, Joe Parent wants to capture the audience's attention right away. He wants to make a vivid, memorable impact on the school board. When it is Joe's turn to speak, he will walk to the podium, take off a shoe, and use the shoe as his prop.

"His shoe?" you ask. What does Joe plan to do with his shoe? Use it like Nikita Khrushchev and pound on the podium?

Overpower the school board with the smell? What in the world does a shoe have to do with fifty-nine teachers being fired? *Nothing.*

That is the whole point. It is a prop used *out of context.* The shoe becomes implausible and out of context the moment Joe takes it off to illustrate his opposition to the firing of fifty-nine teachers. Joe Parent wants to grab the full attention of the audience from the moment he steps up to speak. That is always one of the toughest things to achieve for any speaker — especially so for Joe since he is seventh on a list of ten speakers. Getting the audience's attention is one of the prime reasons why an out-of-context prop is so important. The method may seem weird, but it works.

Other Examples of Props

At a business meeting some props would be effective, others would not:

- An attache case might not be a good prop, but a pair of old sneakers would be.

- A note pad might not be, but a deer head with antlers would be.

- A trash can might or might not be, but a log and saw would be.

- A man's tie might not be, unless of course you weren't wearing a shirt.

- A pen might not be, but a hara-kiri knife would be.

  (Others: a fire extinguisher, a can opener, a corset, a wind-up toy, a rubber ducky, a starter's pistol, a firecracker.)

Notice how, in each example here, the prop is used out of context from its normal surroundings. When you use a prop in this way, it surprises the audience, arouses their curiosity, and ensures that they stay awake to see what happens next.

SELECTING A PROP

There is one more important question to be asked about a prop: "How do I go about selecting a prop?"

Always keep in mind that you must choose a prop that is *out of context* from its usual surroundings. Prowl around your house or office. Gaze out the window. Walk around your yard. Look for something that will raise questions and create wonderment in the mind of the audience, making them ask, "What in the world does this have to do with ... (what you plan to talk about)?" Remember, anything can do the trick, but it is always best to find something provocative to serve as your prop — something unusual, bizarre, or unexpected, or something that might have a story or some drama attached to it.

One final point: Your prop should be large enough so that everyone in the audience can easily identify it.

APPLICATION: With all of the above in mind, the prop I will use is _____

_____

_____

Now that you have a prop, what do you do with it? That is what we explain in the next chapter. We'll show you how to make a Ben Franklin Map for your prop.

However... If You're Conservative

If you think our method is strange or questionable, we ask you to suspend your disbelief and bear with us. For those of you who make important business presentations in which the stakes are extremely high, we ask that you go along with us and learn the method. Then in Chapter 11, we will discuss in detail your particular needs and show you how a more conservative, plausible prop can be used with little or no risk attached. We assure you that when the exercises in this book are completed, you will have created a logical, coherent, interesting, and memorable speech whether you use a plausible or an implausible prop.

4

Make a Ben Franklin Prop Map

You remember Ben Franklin, don't you? He was one of our founding fathers and a very wise man. He developed a simple system to help him make a decision. Ben drew a line down the center of a sheet of paper. On the left side of the line, he listed all the reasons *for* the decision. On the right side of the line, he listed all the reasons *against* the decision. We have taken Ben's method and adapted it to our own needs. We use pluses (+) and minuses (−) to mean *for* and *against*.

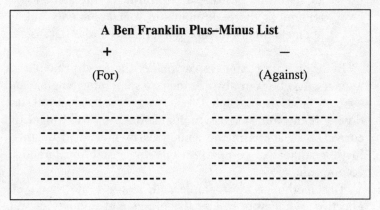

Figure 4.1: A Ben Franklin Plus-Minus List

This array of pluses (advantages) and minuses (disadvantages) helped Ben puzzle through his problem and make a sound decision. We think Ben was on to something when he devised this simple analysis. When you think about it, there are good and bad aspects of everything in the world. Even something as mundane as Joe Parent's shoe has its advantages and disadvantages, its good and bad points. The prop that you choose will also have a large array of pluses and minuses. Here is why they are so important to consider:

1. The pluses and minuses associated with your prop become the material for your talk, which you will use immediately after your opening statements.
2. When we get to the next chapter, we will show you how the pluses and minuses of your prop provide ways, through analogy, to create *persuasion points*, some of which might not otherwise have occurred to you.
3. People remember pictures long after they forget abstract ideas. Your prop and its attributes (+ and −) enhance memory through *the reminder principle*. Since a prop heightens your audience's sensory response, they will remember not only your prop but the advantages and disadvantages (+ and −) associated with it. Best of all, a prop helps the audience remember the main points of your argument; and, not incidentally, it helps you remember your talk.

By using a prop, you employ one of the great principles of memory. You tie your abstract ideas to something tangible and concrete (your prop). Then, later in your speech, when you start driving home your persuasion points, the prop will trigger the correct associations in the audience's memory and tie them to your subject of comparison and the result you intend to accomplish.

This method is very simple and, at the same time, very effective. When you explore the pluses and minuses of your prop, its attributes help you remember your speech. The prop helps anchor your talk in the audience's memory.

To sum up:

- A prop helps you grab the audience's attention.
- A prop helps you create a speech.
- A prop helps you remember your speech.
- A prop helps the audience remember your speech.

Now let's get back to our Ben Franklin Prop Map. As you saw in *Figure 4.1,* a Ben Franklin list of pluses and minuses for a prop is readily understandable and helpful. However, we have pushed Ben's concept one step further and made a map of the pluses and minuses associated with a prop.

WHY A MAP?

A map is a graphic representation of major and minor routes, of possibilities and alternate possibilities. A map lets you see the big picture at a glance. A map is two-dimensional and nonlinear. It allows you to come up with intuitive, nonlogical ideas and, in turn, supports a greater flow of creativity as you analyze your prop. When it comes to stretching the imagination, a map is far superior to a list. It is easy to read. A map makes it easy for you to subdivide and expand ideas; you can easily combine new ideas with thoughts already on the page.

You develop the Ben Franklin Prop Map by writing down:

- What is *advantageous* (+) about your prop
- What is *disadvantageous* (−) about your prop

Keep it understandable. Look at *Figure 4.2* for a blank format of the pluses and minuses associated with a prop. This figure shows you how a Ben Franklin Map differs graphically from a list. Immediately after *Figure 4.2*, we develop several Ben Franklin maps.

Figure 4.2: Comparison of a Ben Franklin List and Map

As you see, the map includes everything that is on the list. The map's added benefits become clearer when you examine the more fully developed example of Joe Parent's shoe (*Figure 4.3*). Notice how the pluses and minuses (+ and −) are displayed. We will outline the steps after *Figure 4.3*.

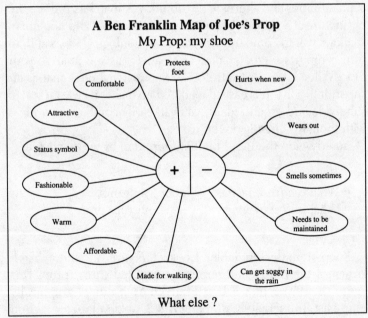

Figure 4.3: A Ben Franklin Map of Joe's Prop

Notice how Joe placed the pluses and minuses on the appropriate sides. He made no attempt to keep the map orderly aside from separating the pluses from the minuses. While he was analyzing his shoe, Joe employed as many of his five senses (touch, taste, sound, smell, sight) as he could to help stimulate more ideas. Finally, Joe added the words *What else?* at the bottom of his prop map. This simple question is a powerful pump primer when creative juices start to run dry. Just focus on any prop point and ask yourself, "What else?" Then wait a bit. When your idea well is indeed dry, move on to the next point.

Here are the six easy steps for the first part of your prop map:

1. Draw a circle in the middle of a blank sheet of paper.
2. Draw a line down through the center of the circle, dividing it in two. Write a plus sign to the left of the line and a minus sign to the right of the line within the circle.
3. Gaze at your prop to consider its pluses, its advantages, its positives.
4. Consider the plus side of the circle first. Write down any idea that pops into your mind. Put it on the left side of the circle. Write only key words or phrases. (A *key word* or *phrase* is simply the core of your original thought.) *Do not edit yourself.* Editing is a later step.
5. Draw a balloon around each key word or thought. Attach a string to the balloon and tie it to the plus side of the circle.
6. Repeat this for the minuses (negatives, disadvantages) associated with your prop. Jot down all your thoughts using key words. Draw balloons around them. Attach a string to each balloon and tie it to the right side of the circle.

Approach the making of a prop map in a playful manner. Generate as many ideas as you can. Go for quantity. Write down every thought — even foolish ones. Don't criticize your ideas; you will evaluate their merit later. Right now, just let your ideas flow. Be sure to leave yourself enough space on the page to expand your ideas. And don't forget to run each plus and minus idea (key word or phrase) through the five senses (how your prop looks, sounds, feels, smells, tastes) to see if they generate more ideas.

Figures 4.4 and *4.5* are additional examples of the six steps we have just taken.

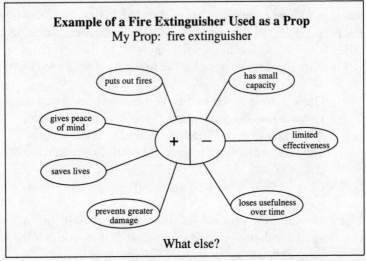

Figure 4.4: Ben Franklin Map of a Fire Extinguisher

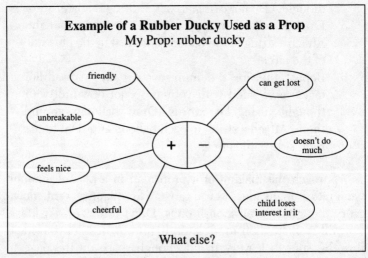

Figure 4.5: Ben Franklin Map of Rubber Ducky

APPLICATION: Now it's your turn. Develop your prop map on a separate blank sheet of paper. Later, you will use it to fashion the points on your persuasion map.

THE FIRST STEP

- Place your prop in front of you.
- Think about its pluses and minuses, its advantages and disadvantages, its good and bad points.
- Write them on the blank sheet of paper, putting the pluses to the left of the circle and the minuses to the right.
- Let your ideas flow.
- Do not edit yet.
- Have fun.

THE SECOND STEP

Now that you have listed all the pluses and minuses of your prop on the Ben Franklin Map, the second step is to expand them. Why? Because you need more material than just key words — otherwise your talk is going to be very short. Also, the prop map becomes the basis for your talk's *beginning*.

QUESTION: How do I expand the prop points on the Ben Franklin Prop Map?

ANSWER: You simply do two things for every prop point:

1. Explain it — what does this mean?
2. Exemplify it — give examples.

In *Figure 4.6*, Joe lists the prop point: "Protects feet."

1. What does this mean? It means the shoe safeguards the foot from dangerous things.
2. Give examples: Stones, glass, thorns, nails, stubbing toe, snow, rain, heat, cold, etc.

Write your explanation and examples — using only key words — below each prop point. Then draw a balloon around the key word or phrase and tie it with a string to the prop point.

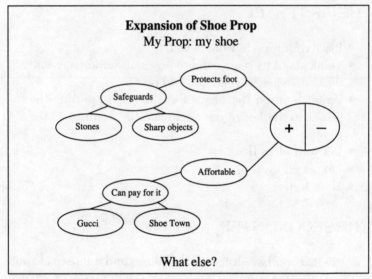

Figure 4.6: Expansion of Shoe Prop

Notice how, in *Figures 4.7* and *4.8*, we take one prop point and expand it using key words.

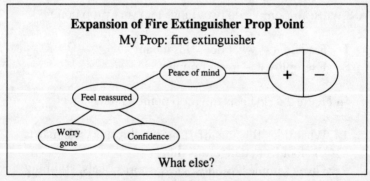

Figure 4.7: Expansion of Fire Extinguisher Prop Point

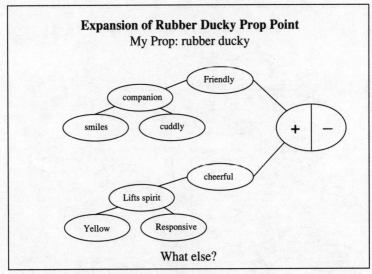

Figure 4.8: Expansion of Rubber Ducky Prop Point

APPLICATION: For practice, take two of your prop points (one plus and one minus) and expand them. Use *Figures 4.7* and *4.8* for guidance.

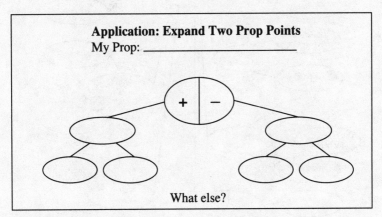

Figure 4.9: Expansion Exercise

For an expanded version of Joe Parent's prop map, look at *Figure 4.10*. It gives you a good idea of how a fully developed Ben Franklin Prop Map looks.

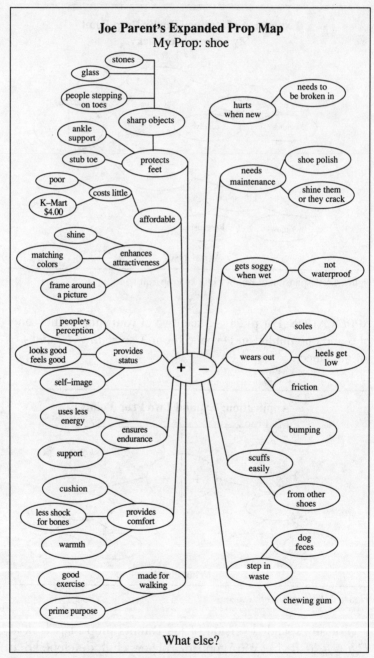

Figure 4.10: Joe Parent's Expanded Prop Map

You see how Joe developed the Ben Franklin Map for his shoe. It is not always necessary to provide an explanation for each plus and minus. As you can see, some of them are so self-explanatory that all you need are examples.

FUNCTION OF STORIES OR ANECDOTES AS EXAMPLES

Everyone loves to be told a story, particularly a good one. When you use stories and anecdotes to expand your prop points, you automatically enrich your talk. Carefully chosen stories help amplify prop points or persuasion points and, at the same time, paint vivid word pictures for the audience. Write down your stories using key words or phrases, then balloon and tie them to the points they elaborate. The use of word pictures, stories, and anecdotes is the best way to elaborate your examples.

APPLICATION: Once again, it's your turn. Take the simple prop map that you created on a separate sheet of paper. Expand each point with examples (and an explanation, if needed) using only key words or phrases.

In the next chapter, we will show you how your expanded prop map connects with the meat of your talk: your persuasion points.

5

Make a Ben Franklin Persuasion Map for Your Intended Result

So far, you have identified your speech's intended result. You have selected a prop and developed prop points through the creation of a Ben Franklin Prop Map. The next step is to decide what you are going to compare your prop *with*. We call this the *subject of comparison.*

QUESTION: What is the subject of comparison?

ANSWER: The subject of comparison is always a person or thing *connected* to the intended result.

Figure 5.1 lists a variety of intended results and shows how Joe Parent's shoe is always compared with something connected to each intended result. In our ongoing *example,* Joe compares his shoe with the teachers who are losing their jobs. The teachers are the subject of comparison. The teachers are connected to the intended result: they are the beneficiaries of the intended result; they are the ones Joe wants rehired.

Other Examples of Subjects of Comparison

Intended Result	Prop	Subject of Comparison
Rehire the teachers	shoe	(is like) *the teachers*
Buy the refrigerator	shoe	(is like) *the refrigerator*
Appreciate Ireland	shoe	(is like) *Ireland*
Vote for me	shoe	(is like) *me*
Join the club	shoe	(is like) *the club*
Read the great books	shoe	(is like) *the great books*

Figure 5.1: Subjects of Comparison

There is an excellent reason why the subject of comparison must be connected to your intended result. A subject of comparison completes the framework (along with your prop and intended result) that enables you to develop persuasion points. At the same time, the subject of comparison keeps you focused on your persuasive goal, preventing you from a slide into rambling digressions. (We know this may seem a little complicated; but bear with us — it will become clear.)

Take a moment now to decide what you will compare your prop with. You can choose anything *as long as it is connected to your intended result.* You will soon discover whether you made a good choice or not. Your ideas will either be fruitful or barren. If they are barren, simply compare your prop with someone or something else that is connected to your intended result. Trust your intuition. It will steer you right most of the time.

APPLICATION: My intended result is _____

_____

My prop is _____

I will compare my prop with something connected to my intended result. My subject of comparison is _____

Now let's combine the prop, the intended result, and the subject of comparison in a Ben Franklin Persuasion Map.

BEN FRANKLIN PERSUASION MAP

As we take you through the steps for creating a Ben Franklin Persuasion Map, you will see how we transfer the prop points over to the persuasion map to jumpstart our imagination. We establish parallels between prop points and the subject of comparison in order to create persuasion points, which in turn helps us to achieve our intended result. The persuasion map looks slightly different from the prop map, but the principles are basically the same.

QUESTION: What are the pluses and minuses (advantages and disadvantages) associated with the result I want my speech to accomplish?

ANSWER: In order to persuade your audience to change to the position you espouse, you must provide them with examples showing what will happen if they *do* change and if they *do not* change. These examples are usually stated in terms of pain and rewards. ("If you do change the way I want you to, you will be rewarded. If you do not change the way I want you to, you will experience pain.")

As we mentioned earlier in the audience analysis, your *persuasion points* should be dictated by your audience's point of view. They always ask: "What's in it for me?" It's what they think that really matters. You cannot sway an audience unless you know precisely what their position is. Once you know their position, then you have a better idea of how they can be rewarded or avoid pain if they change to your position.

Take a look at *Figure 5.2* to see what a blank Ben Franklin Persuasion Map looks like.

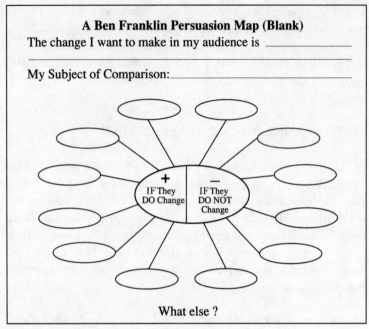

Figure 5.2: Blank Ben Franklin Persuasion Map

Now notice the slight difference between a simple prop map and a simple persuasion map.

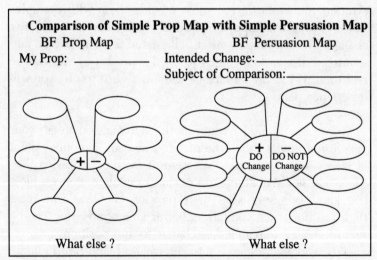

Figure 5.3: Comparison of Prop Map with Persuasion Map

Notice the difference in the cores of the two maps. Since you have already completed the analysis of your prop, you know that *plus* refers to the positives, the advantages associated with the prop; and, you know that *minus* refers to the negatives, the disadvantages associated with the prop. However, on the persuasion map, *plus* refers to the positives, the advantages, the *rewards* your audience will experience when they *do change* the way you want them to. And *minus* refers to the negatives, the disadvantages, the *pain* your audience will experience if they *do not change*.

People are primarily motivated to change for two reasons: either they will be rewarded for making a change or they will avoid pain by changing. Persuasion points developed with this kind of focus touch your audience's hot buttons and motivate them to change.

The quickest way to start the Ben Franklin Persuasion Map is to simply transfer all of your key prop points directly from the prop map to the persuasion map. This establishes important parallels with your prop — parallels you will employ throughout your talk. But just as important, when you transfer the prop points to your persuasion map, they give you an immediate starting place. The hardest part of moving ahead on any complex problem is getting started. So you solve this problem immediately by letting the prop points stimulate your thinking.

In addition, we believe that everything in the universe connects in some way to everything else. When one atom bumps another, the effect is felt around the world, like ever-widening ripples in a pond. Therefore, we think you will enjoy figuring out how your prop points relate to the change you want the audience to make.

The other advantage of transferring prop points to your blank persuasion map is that it saves time. And remember, saving time (without compromising quality) is ASAP's highest priority. Look at *Figure 5.4* to see what we mean.

Joe Parent put his prop map to the left of a blank sheet of paper and transferred all the other prop points — *without* the explanations and examples — to his persuasion map. See *Figure 5.5*.

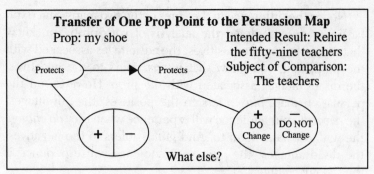

Figure 5.4: Transfer of One Prop Point to Persuasion Map

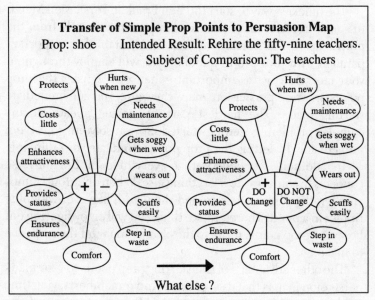

Figure 5.5: Transfer of Simple Prop Points to Persuasion Map

APPLICATION: Follow the example in *Figure 5.5.* Place your Ben Franklin Prop Map to the left of a blank sheet of paper and transfer the prop points — without explanations and examples — to your persuasion map.

Once you have transferred the prop points, your next step is to adapt and expand them.

QUESTION: How do I adapt and expand my *persuasion points,* making them support my *intended result?*

ANSWER: It will be the same for each point. Let's start on the plus side of the map. Ask: "What does this point have to do with the benefits, the advantages, the rewards my audience will experience if they do change the way I want them to?"

For example, on his prop map, Joe Parent had listed *protects* as a positive attribute of his shoe. He transferred *protects* to the persuasion map. He then asked himself, "What does *protects* have to do with rehiring fifty-nine teachers?" As you can see, Joe is comparing this prop attribute (protects) with his subject of comparison (teachers). He thought about it for a moment and decided that if the teachers were rehired, they would continue to protect the children. But protect them how? Joe reasoned that the teachers protect the children from ignorance, from a low standard of living, and from occupational oblivion.

Next, Joe looked at *comfortable,* which he had transferred from his prop map. Once again he asked: "What does *comfort* have to do with rehiring fifty-nine teachers?" He knew these teachers helped their students feel good about themselves. He knew the teachers always fostered good relations among the parents and the school administrators. And he knew these particular teachers had all scored high on a student satisfaction survey. Joe reasoned that these "pluses" would be lost and the community comfort level would be lowered if the teachers were not rehired.

Joe worked through each of the transferred prop points seeking to understand how they might apply to his subject of comparison/intended result and what examples would best illustrate them.

He captured the essence of each persuasion point (by explaining and giving examples) in a key word or phrase, put a balloon around each one and attached it as a subdivision of the persuasion point. This process allowed Joe to adapt and expand each paralleled prop point by finding relevant persuasive examples. Point by point, he was building a strong case to rehire the teachers. Look at *Figure 5.6* for a graphic example of what we have explained.

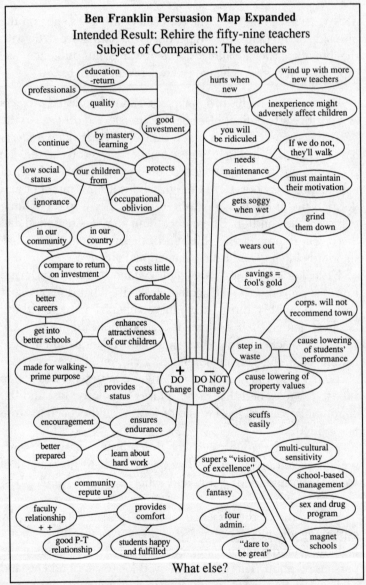

Figure 5.6: Ben Franklin Persuasion Map (Expanded)

APPLICATION: Look at your persuasion map (now that you have transferred your prop points) and begin to adapt and illustrate each point with reference to your subject of comparison. Keep in mind that the audience always asks, "What's in it for me?" Therefore, think in terms of what would reward them if they changed the way you want them to, and what would cause them pain if they didn't change. Ask "What else?" When your ideas peter out, move on to the next category and go through the same process.

QUESTION: What if I come up with some important new ideas on my persuasion map that I haven't included on the prop map?

ANSWER: Simply add them to your persuasion map, along with appropriate examples. Then transfer the new ideas back to your prop map. Transfer *only* the major points — not their explanations and examples. Then think about how these new points apply to your prop and add the examples appropriate to the prop. There is a good reason for this. When you get to your speech later, you will need to have clear parallels between the prop points and the persuasion points.

While Joe Parent was considering the pluses and minuses associated with his subject of comparison and intended result, he realized that "teachers are a good investment." But he had not included an "investment" category on the prop map. So, he simply transferred *good investment* from his persuasion map to his prop map. Using examples appropriate to his prop, Joe started exploring what a good investment had to do with his shoe.

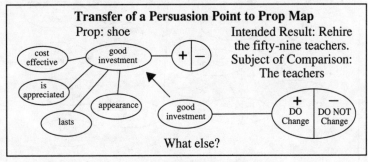

Figure 5.7: Transfer of a Persuasion Point to Prop Map

Now look at *Figure 5.8* to see Joe's fully developed maps:

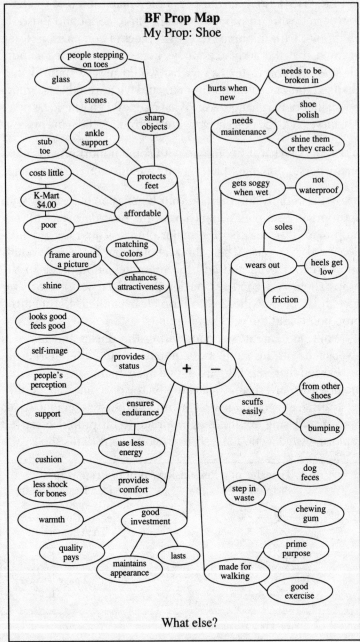

Figure 5.8. Comparison of Prop and Persuasion Maps

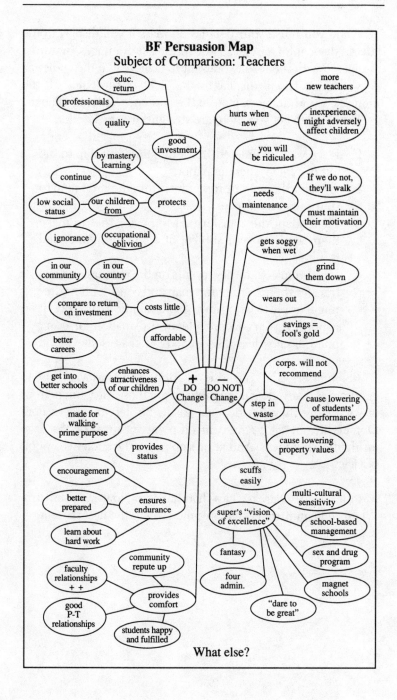

When you finish your persuasion map, it will display to the left of the center circle all the pluses (advantages, rewards) associated with the result you want to achieve — if the audience *does* change. It will display to the right of the circle all the minuses (disadvantages, pain) if the audience *does not* change.

The steps to get you there are straightforward.

1. Place your completed Ben Franklin Prop Map to the left of a blank sheet of paper.
2. Transfer the major prop points from the prop map to your persuasion map.
3. Then adapt the transferred prop categories to make them apply to your subject of comparison/intended result.
4. If you think of any new points on the persuasion map, transfer them to the prop map and consider how they might apply to your prop. As we mentioned before, it is not necessary to provide an explanation for every point. Some ideas (like some truths) are self-evident.

Remember: The purpose of Ben Franklin Maps is to generate as many ideas as possible, to get those ideas out in front of you where they can be seen easily. So, let your ideas flow. Don't edit yourself. Leave yourself plenty of space on the page for the flood of ideas. And always consider the audience's point of view!

APPLICATION: Okay, we have had our fun. Now it is your turn. When you complete both maps, move on to the next section.

6

Bring Order Out of Chaos

If you have completed the applications up to this point, then you have already done the hard part. You have chosen your intended result, your prop, and your subject of comparison. You have completed a Ben Franklin Prop Map and a Ben Franklin Persuasion Map. You now have all the necessary ingredients to make a terrific speech. But first, you have to bring some order to what appears to be chaos.

QUESTION: What *persuasion points* allow me to make my strongest case?

ANSWER: Now that you have completed your persuasion map (and added any new categories that may have popped into your mind), it's time to select your strongest, most persuasive points. Place a checkmark next to the major persuasion points you want to use in your talk. (For an example of what we mean, see *Figure 6.1*.) We suggest choosing only four or five. In any case, go no higher than seven. More than seven will diminish your effectiveness. You don't want to overload your audience.

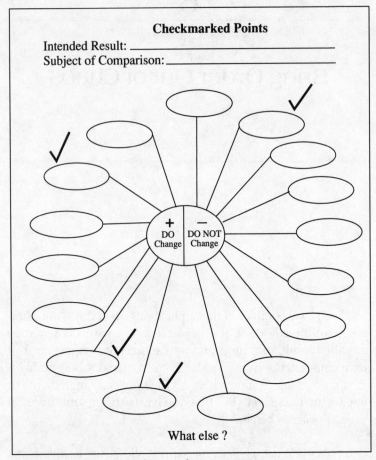

Checkmarked Points

Intended Result: _____
Subject of Comparison: _____

+ DO Change
− DO NOT Change

What else ?

Figure 6.1: Checkmarked Selection of Strongest Points

While you are evaluating and choosing your strongest points, other significant ideas may come to mind. Remember: Creativity is a continuing process; insight can come at any time. Simply snag the thought and integrate it into both the persuasion map and the prop map.

Joe Parent checked four points on his persuasion map.

APPLICATION: Now, select your major points by putting a big checkmark next to the ones you have chosen. Remember: no

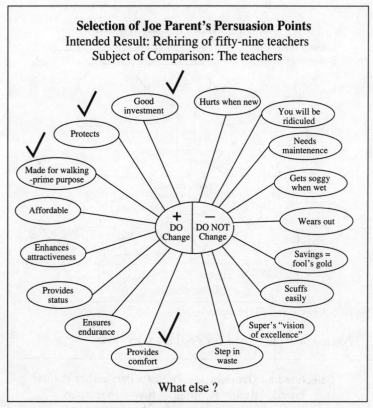

Selection of Joe Parent's Persuasion Points
Intended Result: Rehiring of fifty-nine teachers
Subject of Comparison: The teachers

Figure 6.2: Selection of Joe Parent's Persuasion Points

more than seven! A helpful hint: The checkmarks are easier to see if you use a different colored pen.

Now that you have selected your strongest persuasion points, let's put them in order.

QUESTION: What is the best *order* in which to present my persuasion points?

ANSWER: Your *most important* point should go first. Then the *next* most important, and so on, until you get to the last and least important point.

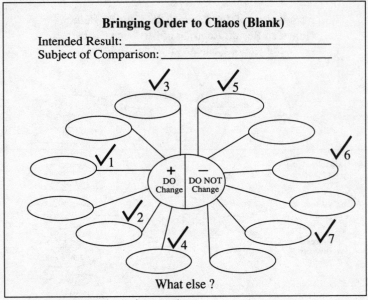

Figure 6.3: Ordering of Persuasion Points

Notice how Joe Parent ordered his selections.

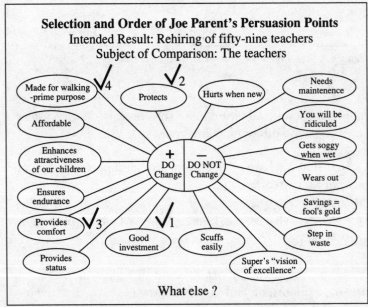

Figure 6.4: Selection and Order of Joe Parent's Persuasion Points

APPLICATION: Your turn. Number your choices on the persuasion map using a different colored pen.

SELECT AND ORDER YOUR PROP POINTS

QUESTION: What *prop points* relate directly to my *persuasion points?* What is their *order?*

ANSWER: The way you select and order your persuasion points dictates how you will select and order your prop points. You need to have parallels between the persuasion points and the prop points. Each major persuasion point must correspond with each major prop point. (See *Figure 6.5.*) If you have a point like "protects" on the persuasion map and you select it to be number two in importance, then you must make "protects" number two on the prop map. There is a strong reason for this symmetry. It makes it easy for you *and* your audience to remember your message points.

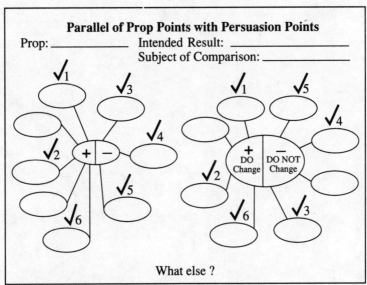

Figure 6.5: Prop Points Paralleled with Persuasion Points

APPLICATION: Select and order your prop points, paralleled with your persuasion point selection and order.

7

Make an Outline for Your Prop and Persuasion Points – Bridge Them

Now that we have brought a certain amount of order to the chaos, we need to arrange our selections in a form that will be easy to speak from. While Ben Franklin Maps are great for stimulating ideas, they are a little confusing when used as podium notes. Consequently, we suggest you make an outline.

An outline is still part of the creative process. In fact, a good idea or a great insight can occur at any time, even while you are delivering your talk. Stay flexible and give each new thought due consideration as it bubbles up.

Once you begin putting your ideas into an outline form, it is all right to mix and match balloons and subdivisions. Just keep the parallels straight between your prop and your subject of comparison. Add anything new that you feel is important, as long as it is coherent and focuses on your intended result.

QUESTION: What will my outline look like?

ANSWER: Your outline is simply a summary — a linear ordering of the most important points. Look at your prop and persuasion maps; then list the selections from each map in the order you have just given them. Be sure to include your explanations and examples using key words or phrases. See *Figure 7.1* for Joe Parent's outline.

Outline of Joe Parent's Prop Points and Persuasion Points
Intended Result: Rehiring fifty-nine teachers

Prop Points (My shoe)	Persuasion Points

1. Good investment
—quality pays
  a. lasts
  b. maintains shape
  c. luster and appearance
  d. affordable
	1. Good investment
	—high return for cost
	  a. quality education
	    for our children
	  b. solid achievements
	  c. saving = fool's gold
	  d. superintendent's spurious
	    "Vision of Excellence"

2. Protection
—safeguards foot
  a. stones
  b. sharp objects
  c. others stepping on toe
	2. Protection
	—safeguards children
	  a. from ignorance
	  b. unemployment
	  c. low social status
	  d. menial occupation
	  e. gets them into college

3. Comfort
—makes walking easy
  a. gives support
  b. speed
  c. helps endurance
  d. warmth
  e. feels good
	3. Comfort
	—children with teachers
	  a. student satisfaction
	  b. harmony
	    principal—teacher
	    teacher—parent
	  c. community repute up,
	    property values up,
	    corporations recommend
	    Jefferson

4. Made for walking
—prime purpose of shoes
  a. good for health
  b. good for heart
  c. good for quality of life
	4. Made for walking
	—teacher's prime purpose
	  is to teach
	  a. intellectual life
	  b. love of learning
	  c. enhanced quality of life
	  d. your children's happiness

Figure 7.1: Outline of Joe's Prop and Persuasion Points

Notice the parallels between the prop points and the persuasion points relate only to the numbered categories, not to the examples in the subdivisions.

APPLICATION: Now it's your turn. With your prop and persuasion maps in hand, prepare an outline emulating the example above. Again, keep in mind that good ideas crop up at any time. Feel free to add, subtract, edit, or modify anywhere along the way. You will clean it up shortly.

If you have worked along with us, then you are almost finished. You have already put together about 90 percent of your talk.

We suggest that you go back now and make sure you have paralleled the major points for your prop and your persuasion points. As we mentioned earlier, you need parallels only between the major points, not the explanations and examples. Also note that you will have much more detail under your persuasion points than under the prop points. This gives you an indication of the amount of time you will be spending on the meat of your talk. Of course, that time will vary with each situation. But here is a good model to follow:

- Opening — 1 percent
- Prop Points — 10 percent
- Bridge — 1 percent
- Persuasion Points — 80 percent
- Closing — 8 percent

Using this model, you can see you have already completed most of your speech assemblage. You have your prop points (10 percent) and your persuasion points (80 percent). Next, we show you how to create a bridge between the two.

BUILD A BRIDGE BETWEEN PROP AND INTENDED RESULT

QUESTION: How do I build a *bridge* between my prop points and my persuasion points?

ANSWER: You need to show the audience the connection between your prop and your subject of comparison. When you introduce and discuss your prop, you gain the audience's attention. They may be puzzled, curious, intrigued — even annoyed — but at least they are awake.

Now you need to make it clear to the audience exactly how your prop ties in with your intended result. The bridge is a very important part of your talk. It becomes your linchpin for clarity. The bridge is the second section of your speech. This is the point where you tell the audience what you are going to tell them.

The *bridge* has four parts:

1. The first part of the bridge is always a simple question that asks "What does this _____[your prop] have to do with _____ [your intended result]?"
2. The second part of the bridge answers the question you just asked. It states the purpose of your talk (i.e., the result you are trying to achieve). "It (the prop) has shown me why you have to..."
3. The third part of the bridge is a simple statement of the analogy between your prop and your subject of comparison. ("Like this shoe, teachers...")
4. And fourth, the bridge states the major points of your speech and what order they are in.

The bridge fulfills the classic admonition to speakers, "Tell them what you are going to tell them." The bridge ties the prop to the purpose of your talk. Then the bridge tells what persuasion points you will make and the order in which you will make them.

Joe Parent's Bridge

The question: "Now, what does this shoe have to do with rehiring the fifty-nine teachers who were fired?" (Prop and intended result)

The answer: "This shoe (*hold it up*) has helped me understand why it is imperative to rehire the fifty-nine teachers." (In other words, the answer is what you want the audience to do as a consequence of your talk — your intended result.)

Statement of the analogy: "Because like this shoe, the teachers..."

What points and the order in which you make them: "...are a good investment, they protect our children, they bring about comfort and harmony in our school system, and they enhance our children's quality of life."

That is your bridge. Once you state it, launch your discussion of each major persuasion point with its respective explanation and examples.

Other Examples of the Bridge

Question: Now what does this rubber ducky have to do with improving customer service? (Intended result.)

Answer: This rubber ducky (prop) has helped me understand why we must improve our customer service. (Intended result.)

Analogy: Because like this rubber ducky, good customer service will...

Order of points: ... bring a smile to everyone's face, support smooth relations with customers, and have all of us whistling a happy tune.

⬦ ⬦ ⬦ ⬦

Question: Now what does this goat head have to do with improving productivity?

Answer: This goat head has helped me understand why it is essential for us to improve productivity.

Analogy: Because like this goat head, failure to improve productivity will lead to...

Order of points: ... increased competition for scarce resources, evaporation of opportunity, and eventually, death.

Notice in these bridge examples that although the intended result is greater productivity, the focus is on the *problems* and *pain* that will result if productivity is not improved.

Question: Now what does this umbrella have to do with training salespeople?

Answer: Actually, this umbrella has helped me understand why it is imperative for you to train your sales staff.

Analogy: Because like this umbrella, sales training can give you ...

Order of points: ... protection in economic storms, comfort in adversity, and give your salespeople the courage to go into any market.

◊　◊　◊　◊

Question: Now what does this centipede have to do with public speaking?

Answer: This centipede has helped me understand why you have to raise your skill level to a habit.

Analogy: Because like this centipede, who cannot walk if he has to stop and think about it, habitual skill at public speaking...

Order of points: ... affords progress, effectiveness, and allows you to achieve the results you intend.

◊　◊　◊　◊

Question: Now what does this bowl of guppies have to do with decommissioning a nuclear reactor?

Answer: These guppies have helped me understand why it is essential to decommission this reactor now.

Analogy: Because like these guppies, this reactor...

Order of points: ... eats its own young, creates fear and turmoil in the community, and will give us peace and harmony only if we remove it from the community.

APPLICATION: Once again, it's your turn.
Complete your bridge using the four-part model.

Question: _____

_____

_____

Answer: _____

_____

Statement of the analogy: _____

_____

_____

What points and in what order: _____

_____

_____

Only two more parts to go! We are almost there!

8

Beginning and Ending

So far we have concentrated on the middle of our speech. We have come up with the pluses and minuses for our prop and the pluses and minuses for our intended result. We have selected our most important points (no more than seven) and listed them in order of importance. We have devised a bridge that spans the gap between our prop and our intended result. We have completed the hardest part! Ninety-one percent of your talk is done. All we need now is a beginning (1 percent) and an ending (8 percent).

QUESTION: What does my *beginning* look like?

ANSWER: We are sure you have been told all sorts of ways to begin a speech: jokes, questions, stunts, quotations, startling facts, and so on. They are all effective. The purpose of any speech beginning is to get the audience's attention. And that is a major reason (but not the only one) why you use a prop.

We suggest only *one* way to begin your ASAP speech: introduce your prop. Since your prop is out of context from its usual setting, it will immediately arouse the audience's curiosity and attention.

HOW TO INTRODUCE YOUR PROP

You simply introduce your prop by holding it up before the audience and saying: "Tonight I want to talk about [my prop]."

Then pause three seconds to let the idea of the prop sink in. Now add: "In a moment I'll show you what [my prop] has to do with [my subject], but right now, I want you to look at this [prop]."

Your second sentence is quite important. While the audience's attention may be aroused by your prop, you need to assure them that you are not speaking frivolously. By stating "In a moment I'll show you what [my prop] has to do with [my subject] ...," the audience will understand you are not simply toying with them and be more kindly disposed to listen to what you have to say about your prop.

After you introduce your prop, proceed with the discussion of your prop points.

This is how Joe Parent begins his talk:

"This evening, ladies and gentlemen, I want to talk about my shoe." [pause three seconds]

"In a moment, I will explain what this shoe has to do with rehiring the fifty-nine teachers who were just fired. But first, let me focus on my shoe."

Other Examples of Beginnings

"This morning, I want to talk about the noble cigar. (pause three seconds) In a moment, I will explain what a cigar has to do with product development. (pause) Right now, take a look at this cigar." ❖ ❖ ❖ ❖

"This afternoon I want to talk about this rubber ducky. (pause) In a moment, I will show you what it has to do with improving customer service. (pause) Right now, take a look at this rubber ducky."

❖ ❖ ❖ ❖

"This evening, ladies and gentlemen, I want to talk about these guppies. (pause) In a moment, I will show you what they have to do with market share. (pause) Right now, take a look at these guppies."

As you can see, the beginning is quite simple.

APPLICATION: Now it's your turn:

The beginning of my talk will be _____

_____

_____

_____

_____

END WITH "PAIN," "REWARD," "CALL TO ACTION," AND "LINK"

QUESTION: What will my *ending* look like?

ANSWER: Traditionally, the end of a speech is what audiences remember best. They remember the beginning of a speech next best. Audiences remember best what they hear last and what they hear first.

With the ASAP method, audiences remember *most* of what you say since you anchor your persuasion points in their memory by the use of a prop. However, since the end of a speech is what audiences remember best, you need to take advantage of that by reinforcing your persuasion points. And you reinforce your persuasion points by presenting them in terms of pain and rewards. These are the two great motivators. Farmers have known this for centuries. They kept their horses pulling the plow by the use of a whip and a carrot.

However, keep in mind that no matter how much people may like reaping rewards for their actions, they act quicker to avoid pain. Here is how to use the pain-reward principle in your ending:

1. Start with the word *if* and state three points that suggest what pain the audience will experience if they do not change.
2. Proceed with the word *when* and state three rewards (benefits) the audience will gain when they do change.

3. Plainly and clearly *direct* the audience to do what you
    want them to do (your intended result).
4. Link your subject of comparison to your prop.

QUESTION: What is the formula?

ANSWER:

1. Start your ending with: "In conclusion ..." We know
    you have probably been told never to end a speech
    with "in conclusion ..." However, a wonderful thing
    happens when you use these two magic words. No
    matter where your listeners' minds may have been
    wandering, no matter how deeply asleep they have
    been, they wake up and pay close attention. They
    know your talk will soon be over and they can lead the
    applause. (We have known some speakers to say "in
    conclusion ..." in the *middle* of their speeches just to
    regain the audience's attention.)
2. Follow "In conclusion ..." with "I'd like to leave you
    with a few thoughts." Then list three examples of pain
    the audience will encounter if they do not follow your
    suggestions and change.
3. After you list their pain options, say: "On the other
    hand ...," and follow that with three rewards the
    audience will gain when they do change the way you
    intend.
4. Then tell the audience exactly what you want them to
    do. Restate your intended result.
5. And finally (in conclusion) make one last link be-
    tween the subject of comparison and your prop.

Here is how Joe Parent ended his speech:
"In conclusion, ladies and gentlemen of the school board, I
would like to leave you with a few thoughts:

IF you do *not* rehire these fifty-nine teachers, then ...

you are choosing to receive the town's ridicule for embracing a
slippery promise over stark fact.

You are choosing 'pie in the sky' over your children's future.
You are choosing to walk these teachers right out of our town —
permanently.

"On the other hand...

WHEN you rehire these fifty-nine teachers...

you will be voting 'yes' to continue quality education in
Jefferson.
You will be voting 'yes' for your children's future.
You will be voting 'yes' for our community's reputation and a
continued increase in the value of your homes.

"Ladies and gentlemen of the school board, there is only one
course of action that makes any sense: rehire these fifty-nine
teachers.

"And one final thought: Tonight, (pause) when you take off *your*
shoes — remember the teachers!"

Another Example of the Ending

"In conclusion, let me leave you with a few thoughts:

If you decide *not* to train your salespeople, then...

you are choosing to allow your representatives to remain
unfocused and to produce at far below their capacity.
You are choosing to allow your salesforce to represent you
in a catch-as-catch-can manner.
You are choosing to disregard the importance of market
share to your business.

"On the other hand...

When you take our sales training...

your salespeople will improve sales by at least 25 percent.
Your salespeople will keep your customers forever.
Your salespeople will increase market share dramatically.

"Ladies and gentlemen, I know you want the best training program for your salespeople. All we need to establish is the starting date.

"One final thought: The next time you open your umbrella to keep away inclement weather — think of your salespeople."

ANAPHORA

Notice in these examples how we use a rhetorical device called *anaphora* (ah-NAFF-orah). The *Oxford English Dictionary* calls an anaphora "The repetition of the same word or phrase in several successive clauses."

In Joe Parent's example, you can see how he uses the anaphora "you are choosing...," which he repeats three times as he warns the school board of the pain they will experience if they do not rehire the teachers. Joe uses a second anaphora ("You will be voting yes...") to remind the school board of the rewards that will come their way when they rehire the teachers.

Why do we suggest you use anaphoras? All the great orators of the ages have used them. They realized that anaphoras helped them build their speeches to an emotional crescendo as they rhythmically hammered home their points. Think about the great speakers of our own age: Winston Churchill ("We shall fight them on the beaches, we shall fight them on the landing grounds, we shall fight them..."), Martin Luther King ("I have a dream..."). These men and their illustrious predecessors knew how effective anaphoras could be. (Abraham Lincoln's "... we can not dedicate — we can not consecrate — we can not hallow — this ground.")

Anaphoras strengthen the ending of any speech. They not only enable you to end your talk dramatically, they emphasize the importance of your call to action (what you want the audience to do). Anaphoras also help to sharply illuminate the final linkage between your prop and your subject of comparison, reinforcing their connection and ensuring that the audience remembers your talk. Notice, too, the use of *if* and *when*. Use *if* with pain, *when* with reward.

A KINDER, GENTLER SPEECH

There may be times when you will want to leave out any reference to the pain or punishment associated with your intended result and focus only on the benefits, the rewards. Perhaps you simply want the audience to appreciate your subject a little more. That is fine. Leave out the threat of pain. However, in cases where you intend to move people to action, it is worth spelling out for them not only the rewards, but the pain they will encounter if your call to action is left unheeded. In either case, continue to package your conclusion in an anaphora. It always gives your speech a strong dramatic ending.

APPLICATION: Now it's time for you to put together your ending.

My ending: ˙
"In conclusion, I want to leave you with a few thoughts.

"*If* you choose not to [Pain, if they *do not* change — preceded by an anaphora] _____

_____

_____

"On the other hand,
When you [Rewards, if they *do* change — preceded by an anaphora] _____

_____

_____

"Ladies and gentlemen, there is only one course of action that makes any sense: ["Tell them what you want them to do" — your intended result] _____

_____

_____

"And one final thought. Tonight [or another time reference], when you [Final link with your prop] _____

_____

_____

You now have the necessary elements of your speech. All that remains is to outline it.

9

Put All the Elements of Your Speech into an Outline

Your speech now has a beginning, bridge, middle, and an ending. All we have to do is bring them together in a logical or sequential way.

QUESTION: What does a simple coherent outline look like?

ANSWER: Your outline captures the main points of your talk from beginning to end using key words that remind you of the details associated with each concept.

OUTLINE

    TITLE
  I. BEGINNING
     A. Tonight — my prop
     B. Later — connection to topic
     C. Right now — my prop

D. Prop points
  1. Point
     a. explanation
     b. examples
  2. Point
     a. explanation
     b. examples
  3. Point
     a. explanation
     b. examples
II. BRIDGE
  A. Question
  B. Answer
  C. Statement of analogy
  D. What points and in what order
III. MIDDLE
  A. Persuasion points
     1. Point
        a. explanation
        b. examples
     2. Point
        a. explanation
        b. examples
     3. Point
        a. explanation
        b. examples
IV. ENDING
  A. "In conclusion, I want to leave you with a few thoughts."
  B. Examples of pain: *If* they do not change, followed by an anaphora and three pains.
  C. "On the other hand ..." Examples of reward *when* they do change, followed by an anaphora and three rewards.
  D. Tell the audience what to do (your intended result). "There is only one course of action that makes any sense..."
  E. Final link between your prop and the subject of comparison. "And one final thought..."

This outline presents you with a structure you can use for any speech. We suggest you study it carefully, then move on to Joe Parent's example.

JOE PARENT'S OUTLINE:

TITLE: Rehiring Fifty-nine Teachers
I. BEGINNING
   A. Tonight — my shoe
   B. Later — connection with rehiring the teachers
   C. Right now — my shoe
   D. Prop points
      1. Good investment
         a. Quality pays
         b. Examples
            i. lasts
            ii. maintains shape
            iii. luster and appearance
            iv. affordable
      2. Protects
         a. Safeguards
         b. Examples
            i. stones
            ii. sharp objects
            iii. others stepping on toes
      3. Provides comfort
         a. Makes walking easy
         b. Examples
            i. gives support
            ii. speed
            iii. helps endurance
            iv. warmth
            v. feels good
      4. Made for walking
         a. Prime purpose of shoes
         b. Examples
            i. good for heart
            ii. good for health
            iii. good for quality of your life

II. BRIDGE
   A. Shoe — rehiring teachers?
   B. Why — imperative to rehire them!
   C. Like my shoe
   D. Teachers
      1. good investment
      2. protect our children
      3. provide comfort and harmony
      4. enhance the quality of life

III. MIDDLE
   A. Persuasion points
      1. Good investment
         a. High return for what it costs
         b. Examples
            i. quality education for children
            ii. solid achievements
            iii. savings = fool's gold
            iv. super's spurious "Vision of Excellence" — four new administrators, multi-cultural sensitivity?, magnet schools?, "Dare to be Great"?, school board management?, sex and drug program?
      2. Protects
         a. Teachers protect our children from
         b. Examples
            i. ignorance
            ii. occupational oblivion
            iii. unemployment
            iv. low social status
         c. Teachers protect by mastery learning
         d. Examples
            i. finest colleges
            ii. good jobs
      3. Provides comfort
         a. Our children are comfortable with teachers
         b. Examples
            i. high student satisfaction

          ii.   harmony: principal–teacher,
                teacher–parent
         iii. community reputation up
         iv. real estate values up
          v. corporations recommend

4. Made for walking
   a. Teachers' prime purpose is to teach
   b. Examples
      i.   intellectual life
     ii. love of learning
   iii. enhanced quality of life
   iv. your child's happiness

IV. ENDING ("In conclusion...")
  A. Pain — *If* you decide not to rehire fifty-nine teachers, you are choosing:
    1. Ridicule, slippery promise, stark facts
    2. Pie in sky, children's future
    3. Walk teachers out of town — permanently!
  B. "On the other hand..." Reward — *When* you rehire these fifty-nine teachers, you will be voting "yes":
    1. To continue quality education in Jefferson
    2. For children's future
    3. For community's repute and increased home value
  C. Result ("Only one course of action that makes any sense...")
  D. Final link (Shoe) Remember our teachers!

APPLICATION: Now it's time for you to put together a coherent outline for your speech. Be sure to refer to the models above.

10

Put It All Together

We are almost there. You now have your outline, but you need to be able to speak from it in an effective manner.

QUESTION: How do I talk from my outline?

ANSWER: Remember how we structured the bridge? We began by asking the question "Now what does this [prop] have to do with [my intended result]?" That is exactly how you should approach your prop points and persuasion points.

USE A QUESTION AND ANSWER FORMAT

A question and answer format is the easiest way to elaborate anything. It also helps you remember your points and keeps you focused. Take a look at Joe Parent's prop and persuasion points. Remember: this is the *middle* of the talk.

Outline of Joe's Prop Points and Persuasion Points with Question Marks

II.   MIDDLE
   A.   Prop points
      1.   Good investment?
         a.   Quality pays
         b.   Examples
            i.   lasts
            ii.   maintains shape
            iii. luster and appearance
            iv.   affordable
      2.   Protects?
         a.   Safeguards
         b.   Examples
            i.   stones
            ii.   sharp objects
            iii. others stepping on toes
      3.   Provides comfort?
         a.   Makes walking easy
         b.   Examples
            i.   gives support
            ii.   speed
            iii. helps endurance
            iv.   warmth
            v.   feels good
      4.   Made for walking?
         a.   Prime purpose of shoes
         b.   Examples
            i.   good for heart
            ii.   good for health
            iii. good for quality of your life
   B.   Bridge
      1.   Shoe — rehiring teachers?
      2.   Why? Imperative to rehire them!
      3.   Because, like my shoe...
      4.   Teachers — good investment
                     — protect our children
                     — provide comfort and harmony
                     — enhance the quality of life

C. Persuasion points
　　1. Good investment?
　　　　a. High return for what it costs
　　　　b. Examples
　　　　　　i. quality education for children —
　　　　　　　 quality professionals
　　　　　　ii. solid achievements
　　　　　　iii. savings = fool's gold
　　　　　　iv. superintendent's spurious "Vision
　　　　　　　 of Excellence"
　　　　　　　　— four new administrators?
　　　　　　　　— multi-cultural sensitivity?
　　　　　　　　— magnet schools?
　　　　　　　　— "dare to be great?"
　　　　　　　　— school board management?
　　　　　　　　— sex and drug programs?
　　2. Protects?
　　　　a. Teachers protect our children from
　　　　b. Examples
　　　　　　i. ignorance
　　　　　　ii. occupational oblivion
　　　　　　iii. unemployment
　　　　　　iv. low social status
　　　　c. Teachers protect by mastery learning
　　　　d. Examples
　　　　　　i. finest colleges
　　　　　　ii. good jobs
　　3. Provides comfort?
　　　　a. Our children are comfortable with
　　　　　 teachers
　　　　b. Examples
　　　　　　i. high student satisfaction
　　　　　　ii. harmony: principal–teacher,
　　　　　　　 teacher–parent
　　　　　　iii. community reputation up
　　　　　　iv. real estate values up
　　　　　　v. corporations recommend
　　4. Made for walking?
　　　　a. Teachers' prime purpose is to teach

  b. Examples
        i.   intellectual life
       ii.   love of learning
      iii.   enhanced quality of life
      iv.   your child's happiness

Notice there is a question mark after each prop and persuasion point. The question mark indicates that you should introduce that point in the form of a question. For example, Joe introduces one of his points by asking, "In what way do teachers protect our children?" You can take virtually any of your prop and persuasion points and precede them with phrases like:

- "What do I mean by...?"
- "How does...?"
- "In what sense does...?"
- "Why does...?"

Then you answer your own question by giving an explanation and listing the examples. A question and answer technique is always more effective than simple declarations. Questions challenge the audience and help keep them attentive.

Let's go back to Joe Parent's speech for a moment. After he lists the four prop points in his opening, Joe moves to his first point, "investment," and asks: "Why is this shoe a good investment?" Then Joe answers this rhetorical question by giving an explanation and examples for "investment." He uses the same question and answer format for each succeeding prop point.

When Joe begins his persuasion section (after the bridge) he asks: "Just as this shoe is a good investment, in what way are the teachers a good investment?" And again he answers his own question by giving an explanation and examples.

Always introduce each new point by asking a question about it. Then use the explanation and examples to answer your own rhetorical question. Asking questions is a great teaching tool (remember Socrates?). And you are better able to persuade people if you begin by asking questions.

The steps are the same for prop points or persuasion points:

1. Ask a question about each point.
2. Answer the question with explanation and examples.

The examples can include stories, anecdotes, humorous asides, anything you choose — just as long as they stick closely to your subject and further your persuasive thrust. The examples should include sufficient background information to insure that the audience knows enough about your subject to be persuaded.

If you want to have a really interactive session, we suggest that you not make the questions rhetorical but actually try to elicit answers from the audience. This is an extremely effective way to hold their attention. The more you can get the audience to participate, the more involved they will be and the better they will remember your talk.

If you are reluctant to ask the audience to respond, afraid that your speech will get out of hand, just remember that only you know where you are going with each point. Since you know your goal, it is easy to direct the audience's attention back toward your intended result. Besides, if your subject is well thought out, their answers will probably not stray too far from your own. And it is possible that some of their answers might even illuminate points better than your own examples.

APPLICATION: Place your outline in front of you and put a bold question mark after each prop and persuasion point.

Now let's take a look at the transcript of Joe Parent's speech. We have placed notes in parentheses to remind you of the various steps of the ASAP method.

TRANSCRIPT OF JOE PARENT'S SIX-MINUTE SPEECH

"This evening, ladies and gentlemen, I want to talk about my shoe. (pause three seconds) (Introduce prop and display it)

"In a minute, I will explain what this shoe has to do with rehiring the fifty-nine teachers who were just fired. But first, let me focus on my shoe. (pause) (Assert prop's relevance)

"This shoe performs some important functions for me. It is a good investment, protects my foot, is comfortable, and it is made for walking. (Note your prop points and their order)

"First of all, (beginning of question–answer format) why is it a good investment? Although this shoe cost $50 — so did the other one, by the way — it is an axiom that you have to pay for quality. You buy cheap, you get cheap. This is a quality shoe, and it will last. It will maintain its shape and luster, its appearance and serviceability for ten years or more.

"Second, how does it protect my foot? This shoe safeguards my foot from injury — from splinters, broken glass, and any sharp objects I might walk on.

"Third, how does it provide me comfort? Every day I am on my feet ten to fourteen hours. This shoe, and its mate, give me support, which in turn gives me endurance. They allow me to continue and persevere in my tasks without getting dreadfully tired.

"And fourth, what do I mean when I say this shoe is made for walking? Well, I think *that* is the prime purpose for which this shoe was created. Not only does walking get you somewhere, but, as you know, it is the best exercise. It is good for your heart, your health, and the quality of your life.

"Now, what does this shoe have to do with rehiring the fifty-nine teachers who were fired? (bridge question)

"This shoe (holds it up) has helped me understand why it is imperative to rehire the fifty-nine teachers. (bridge answer)

"Because like this shoe, these teachers are a good investment. These teachers protect our children. They bring about comfort and harmony in our school system. And they enhance the quality of life for the full lifetime of our kids. (List persuasion points in order)

"We have established that this shoe is a good investment, but in what way are the teachers a good investment? (Reference to prop point and question) These teachers are all seasoned, quality professionals, as their performance reviews clearly show. Quality teachers mean quality education for our children. If we do not rehire these teachers, it is a vote not for education, but for educational bureaucracy, and a slap in the face to our children.

"The money saved by firing these teachers is fool's gold, because it is money that will get redeployed in support of our superintendent's spurious "vision of excellence" — a vision that includes hiring four new administrators at a cost of $250,000. A vision that ignores the solid achievements of these teachers and substitutes vague promises for our children's education. What can we expect from his program in multicultural sensitivity, magnet schools, the "dare to be great" consultant program, his school-based management system, and his laughable sex and drug prevention programs?

"Second, I mentioned that this shoe protects my foot. Now, how do the teachers protect our children? (Reference to prop point and question) They protect them from ignorance, occupational oblivion, unemployment, and low social status. They protect them by their focus on mastery learning. They do it by preparing them well for work, for entrance into the finest colleges, as the record shows. Last year our school system scored in the top 20 percent of all the districts in the state. Ninety-five percent of our college-bound seniors were accepted into the first college of their choice. And of those in the commercial and vocational curricula, more employers wanted to hire them than there were students available — strong evidence that quality education is already happening.

"With fifty-nine fewer teachers on board next year, but four new administrators hired who will oversee a hodgepodge of consultants, programs, and dreams, I think our children will not have been well protected by this decision. Who knows what injury will result? I ask you to please protect us from our superintendent's "vision of excellence," because demonstrated achievement will be sacrificed on the altar of fantasy.

"Third, I said this shoe gives me comfort. How do these teachers provide comfort? (Reference to prop point and question) Well, our children are comfortable with them. The annual student satisfaction survey of teachers shows, across the board, that our children are comfortable dealing with the teachers — find them approachable, that the teachers are *there* when the kids need to talk about a problem. Also, the relationships between the principals and the teachers, and the parents and the teachers have never been better.

"This reputation for harmony in the schools and for quality education has gained the town a wonderful reputation, to such an extent that property values are up — even in a declining market — and corporations are advising their relocated executives to buy homes in our town. With so much unwarranted stress for our teachers, our town's reputation for enlightenment is being jettisoned in favor of the latest ivory tower buzzwords. The result will be discord, overcrowded classrooms, administrative paper blizzards, and too few teachers trying to do far too much. This argues not for excellence but for mediocrity.

"And last, just as this shoe is made for walking, the prime purpose of our teachers is to teach. What do I mean? (Reference to prop point and question) In the course of this educational process, these teachers are turning our children on to the intellectual life and a love of learning. We are all aware of how physical exercise enhances the quality of our lives. Well, the love of learning — that splendid mental exercise — that our children have acquired from these teachers will have consequences that will enhance the quality of their lives for the rest of their lives. Tell me, is there anything more important to you than your children's well-being and happiness?

"In conclusion, ladies and gentlemen of the school board, I would like to leave you with a few thoughts. (The ending is always this way)

"*If* you choose *not* to rehire these fifty-nine teachers, then: (Starts with the pain experienced if they do not change)

"You are choosing to face public ridicule for embracing slippery promises over stark facts. (Note the first anaphora — "you are choosing" — and its repetitions)

"You are choosing pie in the sky over your children's future.

"And,

"You are choosing to walk these teachers right out of our town — permanently.

"On the other hand, (the rewards experienced when they do change)

"*When* you rehire these fifty-nine teachers,

"You will be voting 'yes' to continue quality education in Jefferson. (second anaphora — "you will be voting 'yes'" — and its repetitions)

"You will be voting 'yes' for your children's future.

"You will be voting 'yes' for our community's reputation and a continued increase in the value of your own homes.

"Ladies and gentlemen of this school board, there is only one course of action that makes any sense: Rehire these fifty-nine teachers. (Directive: tell them what you want them to do — intended result)

"And one final thought: Tonight, [pause] when you take off your shoe, remember the teachers!" (Final linkage — prop to result)

Notice how Joe structured his speech using the ASAP format.

ASAP Format

BEGINNING — opening, prop's relevance, prop points in a question–answer format.

BRIDGE — connecting the prop with intended result.

MIDDLE — the persuasion points paralleling the prop points, again in a question–answer format.

ENDING — Reference to pain and first anaphora, reference to rewards and second anaphora, call to action, and final linkage of prop to subject of comparison.

SPEAK FROM YOUR OUTLINE

Joe did not write his speech. He spoke from an outline. We simply included a transcript of what he said. And that is our fervent advice: Do not write out your speech!

"Speak the Speech, I Pray You...!"

You will be infinitely more persuasive if you speak your speech rather than read it. Your personal presence is far more important than burying your head in a script for the sake of turning a well-chiseled phrase. If you speak from an outline you have far more persuasive power than when you wed yourself to a printed text. When you speak from an outline, you are free to use your own feelings, your own particular emphasis and enthusiasm. You can look your audience squarely in the eye and let them know how important your message is to you and to them.

A lot of people read their speeches because they are afraid they will forget, because the speech was written by someone else, or because they have struggled long and hard creating phrases they are now reluctant to give up. Our advice is emphatic: *do not write out your speech. Do not read your speech.*

Perhaps you say: "But it's different every time I rehearse it!" That is okay. The key words are there in your outline to remind you of each point. The key words are in your outline to remind you of the explanation and examples for each point. The key words are in your outline to remind you of your beginning, bridge, middle, and ending. After all, you are the one who put your speech together. You are the one who thought of the explanations and examples. The key words will remind you of what you want to say and you will say it with conviction and aplomb. When you use the ASAP method, you will give a superior speech.

11

However...If You're Conservative

There may be some situations where you would not feel comfortable using an out-of-context (implausible) prop:

- Your career or a lot of money is on the line and you are unwilling to try something new.
- You fear the audience is hostile and might attack you.
- The audience is so conservative that they would be uncomfortable with your method.
- The situation is rigidly structured. The strict rules do not permit an implausible prop to be introduced.

All these reasons are valid. If they make you reluctant to use an implausible, out-of-context prop, we suggest using a *plausible* prop.

PLAUSIBLE PROPS

QUESTION: What is a *plausible prop?*

ANSWER: Any prop that is *in* context, that is, congruous with your theme or subject. To illustrate, let's suppose that Joe Parent felt reluctant to use a shoe (an implausible prop) to convince the school board to rehire the fifty-nine teachers. He felt that a more plausible, in-context prop was needed. What could he use? Here is a partial list:

- A pencil with the point broken off.
- A picture with a professor teaching hundreds of students.
- A sign with the word *rejected* on it.
- A sad child who simply stands beside Joe as he speaks.
- A packet of food stamps.
- A laughing gimmick toy.
- A letter of acceptance to Harvard (last year's) that Joe could burn.
- A star, cut from a foam board.
- A blank teacher's plan book.
- Two books: one well read and dog eared, the other brand new and untouched.
- An attendance sheet showing the students present and the teachers absent.
- An empty teacher's chair.

The list could go on and on, but you see how in each of these instances the prop stands as a symbol of what could happen if the board fails to rehire the fifty-nine teachers.

QUESTION: How do you develop prop points for a plausible prop?

ANSWER: Exactly the same way you would for an implausible prop. Start by making a Ben Franklin Prop Map. As our running example, we will follow Joe Parent again. Let's say Joe chose for his prop the pencil with a broken point. Here is what his prop map might look like.

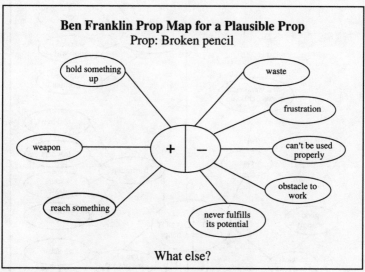

Figure 11.1: Ben Franklin Prop Map for a Plausible Prop

The subsequent steps are also the same:

1. Elaborate your prop points by explaining them and giving examples.
2. Transfer the prop points (unelaborated) to your persuasion map. Just as we explained earlier, you adapt the prop points to the result you intend to accomplish and elaborate them by giving explanations and examples.

Again, let's go back and use Joe as an example. Note in *Figure 11.2* how Joe transferred his prop points to the persuasion map and then elaborated upon them using only key words and phrases.

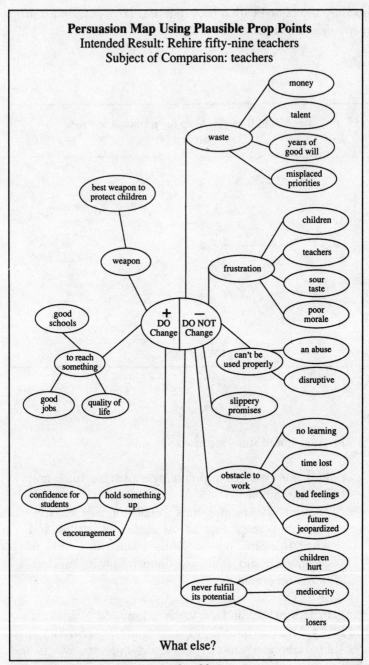

Figure 11.2: Persuasion Map Using Plausible Prop Points

In *Figure 11.2,* Joe graphically illustrates all the pain that will be inflicted on the students, the teachers, and the community if the members of the school board do not change their minds — and some of the rewards if they do.

Notice, too, that Joe emphasizes the negative side of the map. Had he chosen to, he could have elaborated both pluses and minuses equally to create a more balanced view of the prop; or, he could have chosen a different prop that would have stimulated a different emphasis. For example, had Joe chosen the well-planned lesson book from the list of possibilities, he might have used only the plus side of the map. The approach always depends on a blend of what your prop suggests, what persuasion points need to be driven home, and what the speaking challenge calls for.

To continue building a speech with a plausible prop, follow the same path you explored with an implausible prop:

1. You develop a bridge between the prop points and the persuasion points.
2. You use the same opening format.
3. You develop an ending that summarizes your main points by reminding the audience of three pains they will experience or inflict if they do not change and three rewards they will reap when they do change.
4. You call for action.
5. To close the talk, you make a final linkage between the prop and your subject of comparison.

Don Noone recently coached a team of executives from a major corporation who were competing for the contract to build 7,500 collider dipole magnets for the new Supercollider Accelerator in Texas. The stakes were extremely high since the contract was potentially for well over a billion dollars. Each one of the key managers was to give an oral presentation. Don had them make Mind Maps exploring how their corporation was better able to fulfill the requirements of the contract and what they, as individual managers of the corporation, had to offer. Don then asked them to examine their own personal experiences on other large contracts that might offer parallels to the Supercollider Accelerator job.

The quality manager told about his work on the cooling pumps for the U.S. Navy's nuclear submarines. This reminded Don of Tom Clancy's book *The Hunt for Red October.* He had the quality manager go out and buy a copy of the book to use as his prop.

From then on, when it came time for the quality manager to rehearse his portion of the presentation, he stood up before the group, showed them a paperback copy of *The Hunt for Red October,* and said:

"A lot of you have read this book. For those who haven't, it is about a Soviet nuclear submarine trying to elude the U.S. Navy. Now, nuclear submarines make few detectable sounds. But the one way the Navy was able to track Red October was by the sound of its cooling pump. Each Soviet cooling pump makes a signature sound that the Navy can pick up ultrasonically.

"This signature sound creates a unique pattern like finger-prints, so that the Navy can detect the exact class of submarine they are chasing. However, there is a big difference between the Soviet's nuclear subs and ours. We can track Soviet submarines by the sounds their cooling pumps make. But our submarines' cooling pumps make no sound. They cannot be detected ultrasonically. And our corporation makes *all* the cooling pumps for the U.S. Navy submarine fleet."

The quality manager went on to explain the features of a submarine's cooling pump: the exotic material, slight tolerances, 100 percent maintenance-free long life (twenty–thirty years), and the absence of any failures in service. At that point, he told the group that for eight years he had been the quality manager for the cooling pump. He then described parallels between the cooling pump and the collider dipole magnet. The magnet has similar specifications: exotic materials, slight tolerances, 100 percent maintenance-free, long life (twenty-five years), and 100 percent reliability. The quality manager concluded his talk by asserting that the same quality and reliability he and his company brought to the cooling pump project for submarines would be used for the collider dipole magnet.

The quality manager used *The Hunt for Red October* as his plausible prop. It was simple and effective. Most of his audience was familiar with the book. And those who were not were intrigued by the story and the analogy between the story and his proposal. Perhaps an actual model of a cooling pump would have been a more striking prop, but the book was a perfect example of a simple, plausible prop. It immediately grabbed the panel's attention and helped anchor the presentation in their minds.

Incidentally, the management team Don coached won the contract.

Other Examples of a Plausible Prop

President Reagan holding up a three-volume, thirty-five pound report on the U.S. Budget, which he was supposed to read over the weekend.

President Bush holding up a bag of crack as a kickoff for his talk on drugs and crime.

A police chief displaying nine automatic weapons as a launch for his report on gun control.

Saddam Hussein patting a boy hostage on the head for TV coverage (which backfired — an inept use of a prop).

What Is the Benefit of Using a Plausible Prop?

It allows you to put together a talk ASAP, just as you would with an implausible prop. The method is exactly the same. A plausible prop has good and bad points that become the basis for your persuasion points. A plausible prop anchors your talk to something concrete, something continually displayed for reinforcement. You have the same parallels between your (plausible) prop and your persuasion points that help both you and the audience to remember your speech. So, for speed of creation, a plausible prop is a viable way to prepare your talk. It is low risk and puts no demand on your audience's tolerance. It is entirely within their comfort zone as far as logic, congruity, and appropriateness are concerned. And using a plausible prop is far better than using no prop at all.

There are two major differences between the use of a plausible prop and an implausible one. An implausible (out-of-context) prop is much more effective as an attention-grabber. Second, an implausible prop ensures that more of your speech will be remembered. Certainly a plausible prop will work fine in any situation, but an implausible prop has attention-getting power beyond any other method we know. We also know, by virtue of the way the brain works, that an unexpected, surprising, curiosity-arousing, even bizarre prop creates memorable associations with your persuasive points. As a consequence, when you use an implausible prop, the audience will remember your ASAP speech long after they have forgotten all other forms of speeches.

If you are concerned about making a fool of yourself using an implausible prop, we recommend that you try out such a prop in a low-risk speaking situation. We guarantee you will immediately see for yourself what a powerful tool it can be. But until that time, you may want to take a more conservative approach and use a plausible prop. In any case, plausible or implausible, *use a prop.*

PLAUSIBLE PROPS IN SELLING SITUATIONS

Quite often, salespeople have to argue by analogy in order to persuade a prospect (as in the case of the quality manager making an analogous leap from submarine pumps to dipole magnets). This is a perfectly appropriate strategy that is used all the time. However, this strategy would be greatly enhanced if salespeople anchored their product or service to a plausible prop. Indeed, in many instances, the object to be sold becomes the plausible prop (a stove, a car, a house), in which case an analogy is no longer necessary. How does the ASAP method apply to this situation?

1. Know the result — "I want you to buy what I'm selling."
2. Audience analysis — qualify prospects through questions.

3. Ben Franklin Map of persuasion points — note all the pluses, advantages the prospect will reap *if they buy;* note all the minuses, pains, disadvantages the prospect will suffer *if they choose not to buy.*
4. Ending — close by asking for the order ("What color would you like?" "When do you want it delivered?" "How would you like to cover your investment?").

CONCLUSION

You now understand the ASAP method. It works whether you use a plausible or an implausible prop. We suggest you periodically review ASAP's steps so that you always have them fresh in your mind. That way, when you are under some future time-crunch, you will have the confidence and the expertise to produce a terrific speech on short notice — ASAP.

12

Delivery Day

By this time, you have created and clearly outlined your ASAP speech. Once again, we emphasize: *do not write out your speech.* Speak from your outline. Let the key words and key phrases from the outline prompt your memory. If you write out your speech you will be tempted to read it, which is self-defeating, and you will lose your effectiveness. You will not be persuasive. Your real potency as a speaker emerges when you spontaneously speak from an outline. Spontaneity gives you an air of authority that connotes true mastery of your subject matter.

The next step in the ASAP process is to get ready for delivery day. In this chapter, we deal with fear, rehearsal, visualization, room arrangement, acoustics, vocal warm-ups, appearance, nerves, props, and the audience.

This is it: D-Day (Delivery Day). The day the butterflies arrive. The day those nagging fears that you are going to be a total failure start bubbling up to erode your confidence. The day you start wondering if you will be able to remember your own name, much less your speech. It's the day you start asking, "What if they hate me? Worse than that, what if they laugh at me? What will I do?"

But what exactly do we fear when we speak before a group? We fear that we might fail, that we will seem inadequate to our peers. We fear they will find out what is really wrong with us — that we are not very bright or talented or knowledgeable. A lot of us fear we will forget what we are supposed to say.

QUESTION: How can I combat fear?

ANSWER: We can't guarantee you will be free of your butterflies, but we can help you train them to fly in formation. Speaking in public has long led the list of the most feared events in people's lives. But this fear can be controlled by a combination of physical and mental activities.

First, you are never as inadequate as you think. Be assured the audience is just as wrapped up in their own fears and doubts and needs as you are. They will not be spending much time doing a detailed analysis of you. They are far more concerned about themselves. Remember, they always ask, "What's in it for me?" Therefore, if you focus on the audience's needs, not on your own inadequacies, your nerves will be rapidly forgotten. Understand that you *can* control what you focus on; and since you can focus on only one thing at a time, you can control your fear by focusing on the audience.

Second, when you use the ASAP method to create a speech, you have a strong ally, a time-proven structure that works. An ASAP speech is virtually impossible to forget. The key words and key phrases of your outline prompt instant associations between your tangible prop and your more abstract persuasion points, making them remarkably easy to remember.

COMBATING FEAR WITH PREPARATION AND REHEARSAL

An ASAP speech is flexible. Let's say you prepared a twenty-minute speech, but because of last minute time constraints, you were told to cut it down to six minutes. With ASAP there is no reason for panic, no reason for frantic blue-penciling. You retain all your prop and persuasion points and pare down only the explanations and examples. Thus, you would be able to drive home all your points no matter what time frame you are given. While the ASAP speech is flexible and easy to remember, it needs some additional help from you. You need to be prepared. Remember the old Boy Scout motto? It's not bad advice no matter what you are doing. And the best way to be prepared is to rehearse.

Nothing — absolutely nothing — takes the place of rehearsal. Don't think just because you have been speaking all your life you can automatically walk up and give a good speech. It takes practice, just like learning to play the piano, just like golf or tennis. The more you practice the better you become. Athletes know this. Musicians know it. Why do football teams go over basic plays again and again? Why do Broadway shows rehearse four to six weeks and then preview for another month or so? Theater people know you never get it right the first time out. They also know that exciting new discoveries are made during rehearsals. They know the value of rehearsing a show over and over until it becomes precise, because only with precision does it become exciting.

Each new audience causes another batch of butterflies to hatch in actors' stomachs. But actors have learned that butterflies go away a few minutes after the curtain rises. How? They know that only hard work and preparation chase away butterflies, gremlins, and fear monkeys. Therefore, although each night's audience is new and different, the actors rest secure in the knowledge that rehearsal and repetition will again pull them through.

Our strongest counsel for any speaker is *rehearse! rehearse! rehearse!* The biggest enemies of fear are preparedness and a focus on the audience's needs and wants. Remember: you always look more in control than you feel. Audiences rarely notice your little mistakes. Besides, most audiences are used to poor speeches. ASAP gives you a delightful opportunity to surprise them!

QUESTION: How much should I rehearse? And how do I rehearse?

ANSWER: Rehearse as much as you can. But rehearse your speech no fewer than four times!

HOW TO REHEARSE

After you put together your ASAP talk and complete the outline, rehearse it two times. Rehearse anywhere: in your office, while you are jogging, in your shower, or strolling down a country lane. Those of you who spend a lot of time commuting can rehearse driving back and forth to work. We have done that a lot. Just make sure you rehearse your talk out loud. This is important. Expect these two rehearsals to be rough and ill-formed, but continue to plow through to the end. You will undoubtedly come up with new ideas, new things to say, and new ways to say them. Perhaps new stories or anecdotes will occur to you. This is the place to try them out and incorporate them into your outline. Make a note of how long it takes to complete your talk, but don't be too concerned about time now. However, if you planned a six-minute talk and it takes thirty minutes to get through it, then get out your paring knife fast.

We suggest you memorize the shell of your ASAP speech. The shell consists of three parts: the beginning, the bridge, and the ending. Chapter 13 gives you a fully delineated example of the ASAP shell.

The *third* time through, deliver the speech as if you were doing it for real: walk to the podium, display the prop, make your beginning, bridge, and ending strong and sincere. We suggest you videotape this rehearsal. If you do not have a videorecorder, the next best thing is to rehearse in front of a full-length mirror and tape your run-through with a tape recorder. This is the rehearsal that shows you all the places you are saying "er," "uh," "you know?" "right?" and "okay?".

If you videotape the rehearsal, you will perhaps see someone who looks like you but acts like an alien creature from Mars. We can imagine your screams: "That wasn't me. I don't know who that person was, but it wasn't me!" It was you, it is you, and you are not as weird as you think. We all shudder when we see ourselves speaking — particularly for the first time.

Learn from the tape. Learn how you can become more sincere and enthusiastic. Learn how to control your fly-away gestures. Perhaps you need to make larger gestures, rather than those little flipper movements from the fig-leaf position. Time this run-through.

The *fourth* time through is your final dress rehearsal. No mistakes, no stops. Make sure it's the length you want. It is up to you whether or not to tape this rehearsal. Concentrate on being sincere and enthusiastic. You must, of course, believe what you are saying. You must feel it has importance. Otherwise, you will sound indifferent, or worse, insincere. You must convince the audience there is a burning issue here. Forget about snappy opening jokes. Forget about wrapping your mouth around brilliantly sculpted prose. Sincerity, not charm or wit or eloquence, is your most valuable persuasive tool.

Enthusiasm and Confidence

Directly at the heels of sincerity is enthusiasm. Being enthusiastic means you care about what you are saying — you are passionate about it. It is your energy and enthusiasm that will fire up your audience. They will only be as enthusiastic as you are. To be enthusiastic, act enthusiastic.

Don't get lazy. Don't tell yourself, "Aw, it'll work out when I get up there at the podium. I don't need to rehearse. I speak all the time. What's the big deal? I'm sure I'll get inspired by the audience. Besides, I don't want to peak too early!" To that response we say, "Phooey!" and add a couple of Bronx cheers for good measure. That attitude leads the way to mediocrity and ineffectiveness.

If you really want to persuade a group to change — to get you the result you intend — you have to stay ahead of the audience every step of the way. You must surprise and intrigue them. You must be confident of your abilities. The more confident you are, the easier it will be to persuade them. Confidence comes when you are prepared. To be prepared you need to rehearse good material. With ASAP, you have good material. Now rehearse. (Incidentally, if you have time to rehearse more than four times, do it. It can only get better.)

Visualization

We suggest you visualize yourself delivering your ASAP speech to an enthusiastic crowd. These days, visualization is at the frontier of conditioning for athletes. Swimmers visualize every stroke, every turn at the end of the pool. They see themselves winning in record time. Ski racers visualize themselves skiing perfectly through every gate on the slalom course. They visualize how good their form is, how perfectly balanced they are, how they are racing much faster than ever before.

Actually visualize your entire speech. See yourself delivering it. Hear yourself saying the words. Visualize how good it feels to speak spontaneously, prompted only by your outline's key words and phrases. Visualize yourself being sincere, speaking with authority and enthusiasm. Visualize the audience being persuaded to your point of view. Visualize the standing ovation and bravos at the end of your talk.

APPLICATION: What steps will you take to plan this predelivery, preparation, and rehearsal phase? _____

_____

_____

_____

D-DAY HAS ARRIVED

Up to this point, we have discussed what happens before D-Day. Now comes the day you deliver your ASAP speech.

Arrive at the place where you will speak at least an hour early. There is an excellent reason for this. You want to make sure the room is arranged properly. Just as theaters, stadiums, arenas, and churches all have seating arrangements designed to meet their specific purposes, the room in which you are to speak should be arranged to show you off to good advantage.

Preparing the Room

Sometimes the room arrangement cannot be altered. Joe Parent had no control over where he spoke. But 95 percent of the time if you insist you can change the way the room is set up to better enhance your talk. If you contact the people in charge a day or so ahead of time, they are usually quite amenable to any change you wish to make.

QUESTION: How do I arrange a room to enhance my talk?

ANSWER: Just as you are the playwright and main actor, you also need to be the producer, director, and lighting-scenery-costume designer. This is your show. You want to be an unqualified hit. So, insist on what is best for you.

First of all, look at the room itself. You do not want a large room for a small crowd; that would diminish your effectiveness. Check to make sure there will be no loud, disruptive gatherings in the adjoining rooms while you are making your presentation.

Check the seating arrangement. The closer you are to the audience, the better you will be able to persuade them. If the chairs are not secured to the floor, move them so that they form a "C" or a "U" with you in the center (ⓒ). Or better still, an upside-down split "V." (ᴧ•).

Arrange the seating so that the entrance and exit doors are toward the back of the room. You do not want latecomers upstaging you. Put out slightly fewer chairs than you think will be needed. Stack the rest at the back. This way, the crowd will have to fill in the seats down front and latecomers will be forced to sit at the rear. If you are speaking in a room that has permanent theater-type seating, rope off the back area to force the audience closer to you. If you can't change the seating arrangement, do the best with what you have.

If there is a lectern (there almost always is), move it to one side and use it only as a place to put your outline or rest your prop. You want no barriers between the audience and you. When you attend the theater, you don't want anything blocking your view of the stage. It's the same with sporting events. To be your persuasive best, you need to use your whole body and be more than just a talking head peeping over the top of a lectern.

If you are speaking to more than seventy people, you will probably need a microphone. Arrange to be supplied with a hardwired lavaliere mike (one that hangs around your neck) or a cordless hand mike. A lavaliere mike gives you more freedom to use your hands.

Check the lighting. Make sure there is plenty of light on the area where you will be speaking and where your prop is displayed. Remember: you are the star. Stars need to be seen. Make sure you can read your outline in that light.

Check the room temperature. If it is too warm, your audience will nod and droop. Insist that the temperature be kept at 65–68 degrees. The audience is always perkier if the room is a little chilly. If the room is too hot, simply fling open the windows.

As we said earlier, have no barriers between yourself and the audience. Turn the lectern sideways, or better still, use a table for your outline and your prop. You can sit on the table if it's strong enough, or lean on it, as long as you stay beside or in front of it.

Vocal Warm-Ups

As you arrange the seating for your audience, you can also use the time to warm up your voice. Pretend you are a tiny owl that has just been surprised. Start at the top of your vocal range and say "Hoo-o-o-o-o-o" in a descending fashion until you get to the bottom of your vocal range. It should sound something like a bomb dropping. Try to blow air through your nose at the same time. Do not strain. Keep it all comfortable.

When we are nervous, our vocal cords become taut and, as a result, our voices get higher. This startled-owlet exercise causes our vocal cords to loosen and start resonating properly again so that our voices return to their normal pitches.

Alternate the "Hoo-o-o-o's" with a lip articulator. Say: "The tip of the tongue, the lips, the teeth." Repeat it several times aloud, exaggerating the movement of your lips and tongue as you say it. Then go back to imitating the startled owlet.

QUESTION: How should I dress?

ANSWER: Each speaking event varies. The best rule of thumb is "When in Rome ... " We suggest you dress slightly better than the audience. Let your prop be the only out-of-context part of your talk.

While You're Waiting to Go On

You have arrived early. You have set up the room the way you want it. Perhaps you have had time for a mini-rehearsal before the audience starts filing in. If it is appropriate, we suggest you greet people as they enter. This accomplishes two things. It gets your blood moving and your mind off your nerves. And it gives you a chance to meet and talk with your audience beforehand. You get to know them; they get to know you. This increases your chances of persuading them. Try to remember their names. It is always flattering to have your name remembered.

Sometime before you give your talk, take a moment to do a final mirror check. Check your hair, teeth, makeup, and shoes, tuck your shirt back in, (men) check your zipper. Remove any loose change or keys from your pockets, any jangling bracelets, anything that rattles or clanks. If you wear one, also remove the plastic protector, pens, and pencils from your shirt pocket.

If you have to sit around and wait before you speak, your butterflies may start getting feisty again. You can harness them by several methods. The most effective is deep diaphragmatic breathing. Oxygen has an excellent calming effect. Inhale deeply through your nose into your belly as you count to six, hold your breath for six counts, then exhale through your mouth as you count to twelve. Be sure to push all the air out of your lungs.

1. Inhale-2-3-4-5-6
2. Hold-2-3-4-5-6
3. Exhale-2-3-4-5-6-7-8-9-10-11-12

Continue this breathing pattern for several minutes. Make certain you are using diaphragmatic breathing. If the area right below your rib cage swells out as you inhale, then you are breathing correctly. When it is done properly, your chest does not expand — just your belly. Think of breathing all the way down to your toes.

While waiting to speak (if you are not in full view of the audience) you can do several isometric exercises that help to get the blood flowing again. Reach down on either side of you and grab the seat of your chair. Pull up as hard as you can for ten seconds. Then let go and feel the blood flowing warmly into your arms and hands.

Scrunch up your toes as tightly as you can and hold them that way for ten seconds. Release them and feel the warm blood flowing into your feet. Make fists as hard and tight as you can. Hold them for ten seconds. Let go and feel the blood entering your hands.

If you are seated at the head banquet table, you might be tempted to have a glass of wine or two to calm your nerves. We respectfully urge you to stay away from all alcohol, caffeine, or calming drugs such as valium or propranolol. They do not help; they only get in the way.

THE MOMENT ARRIVES

Now comes the time for you to speak. You are introduced. You rise and walk forward with purpose to greet the audience. (We suggest you always write your own introduction and supply it to the person who introduces you. That way you are assured of having everything included. Keep it short, two minutes at most. Bring an extra copy in case the original is misplaced.) When you reach the spot, place your outline on the lectern or table. Make sure you stand up straight with your weight equally distributed on both feet.

When you stand erect, centered, balanced on the balls of your feet, it gives you a dynamic appearance. It allows your gestures to be open and full, your voice to be resonant and convincing. It helps you to look and sound like you mean what you say. It gives the appearance that you own the ground you stand on.

Take a moment to look at the audience. Smile. Hold up your prop. Look at it. Look back at the audience. Say your first sentence. And you are on your way.

During the speech, you can either hold your prop or place it on the table or lectern; but it should always remain in full view of the audience. As you handle the prop, make sure everyone in the audience can see it. Don't always hold it in front of you, but out to the side.

Speak in an energetic, yet conversational way using colorful nouns and kicking verbs. Talk to all the people in the room, but make sure you talk only to one person at a time. Speak to them as if you were speaking to your family — if your family happened to be in the next room. In other words, speak conversationally but ratchet up your volume and energy. Always speak a little louder than you think is necessary.

Communicating to the Audience

Respect your audience. Respect their intelligence. Do not talk down to them. Convince them there is a burning issue here, a reason for change. Be pleasant and sincere and enthusiastic.

Most audiences assemble with hope in their hearts. They anticipate that the concert, the play, the movie, the sermon, the speech will be good. They are already on your side before you even open your mouth. Do not let them down. If you greet them at the door, you are even further ahead since you will be talking to friends, not strangers.

You know a lot more than the audience about your subject. The audience already recognizes that. They expect you to be an expert. Therefore, you should act like an expert. An expert is forthright. An expert speaks sincerely and enthusiastically. An expert looks people in the eye.

A lot has been said about eye contact. We think it is very important. If you never look directly at the audience, you send a signal that belies your message. If you are shifty-eyed, you will be an ineffective persuader. Look directly at each audience member. Hold his or her gaze for several seconds (three or four), then move your focus to someone else. If your eyes light on a grumpy, sour face, do not let it affect you. Look pleasantly at it and move on.

Our whole-hearted suggestion is that you heed the golden rule. Speak to others as you would have them speak to you. You know what kind of speakers you like. Try to be like them. Send out your energy and encompass the audience. They will thank you for it.

APPLICATION: Throughout this chapter we have given you a number of suggestions on how to improve your skills as a speaker. However, we are aware that our book's title is ASAP — as soon as possible. We know that rehearsals and room rearrangements take time. If you do not have the time to adjust room arrangements, you will still do fine. If you do not have time to rehearse, we suggest you drop everything and read Chapter 13 right now. However, even if you have to put together a speech ultrafast, find the time to rehearse. You will be amazed at how much you improve. Now apply what you have learned to your present speaking event:

How will I define my audience? _____

_____

When will I rehearse? _____How will I visualize myself? _____

_____

How will I warm up? _____

_____

How will I arrange the room? _____

_____

How will I dress? _____

_____

13

How to Prepare Your Speech on the Way to the Podium

Suppose you are attending a banquet along with three hundred other guests and suddenly — with no advance warning — you are called upon to speak! This would be enough to send the average person into cardiac arrest. But even if you took up the challenge and somehow avoided heart problems, it is likely that, unless you are a clever improviser, you would bumble your way through pleasing neither yourself nor the audience. When you use the ASAP method to create a speech, you need never be caught off guard again. Once you master the ASAP method, you can literally *prepare your speech on the way to the podium.*

The best way to explain the ASAP method is to walk you through a scenario, annotate the method as we proceed, and finally extract the core of the method, which you can then use in any future circumstance.

SCENARIO

You and your spouse are at a $100-a-plate fundraising dinner for an organization whose mission is to find a cure for muscular dystrophy. In the course of the introductions, the master of ceremonies, without any prior notice, calls you by name and says, "Come up here to the podium and say a few words."

In the past you would have wished for the earth to open and swallow you on the spot. But now that you have mastered the ASAP method and know how to prepare a speech instantly, it is no problem at all.

Lightning fast, before you even open your mouth, you identify the three main elements necessary to build your ASAP speech:

1. *Your intended result* — what you want to accomplish.
2. *A prop* — to support your talk.
3. *A subject of comparison* — to compare with the prop.

You decide that your *intended result* is to get this bunch of fat cats to add another $100 a plate to their donation. You know they can afford it, being one of the fat cats yourself. That takes care of your intended result. Next, you look around for a prop. Your eye lights upon the floral arrangement at your table. That will be the prop you pick up and carry to the podium with you. Finally, you need to decide what you are going to compare your prop with — *the subject of comparison*. The subject of comparison is always a person or thing that is in some way connected to your intended result. In this case, the subject of comparison is the afflicted children who will benefit from additional donations.

Now you have the three elements necessary to build your speech:

1. *Intended result* — additional $100 a plate donation.
2. *Prop* — floral arrangement.
3. *Subject of comparison* — children with muscular dystrophy.

All you need to do now is plug them into the ASAP *shell* — the key sentences applicable to any speech. The following dialogue might then occur (notice we said dialogue — your talk will involve the audience throughout):

"Tonight I want to talk about this arrangement of flowers. (Pause) In a minute I will explain what it has to do with fundraising. Right now focus on these flowers, and if you would, help me out by supplying answers to the questions I'm about to ask: What are some of the pluses and minuses associated with these flowers? As you know, everything in the world has its good and bad aspects. So, what are the good and bad aspects of these flowers? The positives and negatives? What are some of their significant features? Good or bad. Any ideas?"

At first, it might take a little cajoling to get the audience to participate, but soon someone will respond and then the responses will multiply. Just be patient and keep insisting. Possible responses might be

"They're beautiful. They're fragile. They need care. They're cheerful. They make the world beautiful. They die very soon. They are expensive."

What is the audience doing by answering? They are giving you your prop points. In a moment, you will choose two or three of the strongest prop points suggested by the audience. Then, by analogy, these same prop points become your persuasion points — the heart of your message. This step is important because you need to establish a parallel between your prop points and your persuasion points. Let's say, for simplicity's sake, that you chose three attributes of the flower arrangement named by the audience: "beautiful," "fragile," and "needs care."

When you have elicited a sufficient number of responses from the audience, the next step is to make a *bridge* between your prop and your subject of comparison. This is also done in a question–answer format:

"Now, you may be wondering, 'What does this floral arrangement (your prop) have to do with these children afflicted with muscular dystrophy (your subject of comparison)?'

"Just as these flowers are beautiful, fragile, and need care, the children (your subject of comparison) *this organization supports are beautiful, are fragile, and need care."*

Note that the subject of comparison to the prop is "the children" and the children are the beneficiaries of the intended result, that is, increased funds.

"Perhaps you can help me out again. In what sense are these deformed, handicapped children beautiful?"

You once more solicit audience involvement. Wait for their response and listen to what they say. They will tell you in what sense the kids are beautiful. To get audience members to elaborate on their responses, simply ask for an example. When you get enough responses, move to the second point.

"We have said these flowers are fragile…"

Note the reference to your prop.

"But, in what sense are the children fragile?"

Wait, and let the audience tell you.

"We also said the flowers need care and will die if the care is not given. How do these children need care?"

By now the audience is excited about participating and the answers will be coming rapidly. Be sure to repeat the suggestions so all the audience can hear them. After you have received sufficient answers, bring this section to a close. You make a mental note of the strongest points suggested by the audience. Let's say the audience suggested: "stunted growth," "painful rejection," "die too early from lack of care," "can be cured," "can provide proper medical care," and "can live fuller, happier lives," among others.

"In conclusion, I want to thank you for your excellent responses and leave you with a few thoughts.

If this organization does not receive greater support from you, then:

These beautiful, fragile children will be stunted in their growth.

These beautiful, fragile children will experience painful rejection in their lives.

These beautiful, fragile children will die too early from lack of care."

You tell them here of three painful consequences the children might suffer if the audience does not give the organization more generous support. Notice that each pain is introduced by an anaphora — the repetition of a phrase at the beginning of a series of thoughts ("these beautiful, fragile children will...").

"On the other hand,

When you open your hearts and add $100 to your plate,

Your gift will provide these children with a springboard to a cure.

Your gift will provide these children with a springboard to proper medical care.

Your gift will provide these children with a springboard to a fuller, happier life."

Here you remind the audience of three rewards they will reap when they support the organization more generously. Note, too, the rewards are introduced by another anaphora — a thought fragment repeated three times in a row ("your gift will provide these children with a springboard to...").

"Ladies and gentlemen, open your wallets, pull out your credit cards, dust off your checkbooks, and let's make this spontaneous expression of your generosity a three-figured one."

This is the call to action — you tell them explicitly what you want them to do.

"And one final thought: As you look at the beautiful floral arrangements in front of you, (pause) think of our kids!"

This is the final linkage of your prop to your message. And this is what will make it memorable.

That is it. That is your talk. It is a good, effective talk. The audience has been involved. You have moved them to action. And you can bet your talk will be memorable.

THE ASAP METHOD

Now let's go back and winnow out the ASAP method from the scenario. There are five major steps:

1. Know your intended result.

On any occasion when you are suddenly, with no advance warning, called upon to speak, the master of ceremonies will usually give you either a direct or nondirect invitation. In the scenario above, the emcee gave a nondirect invitation ("come up and say a few words") to speak in support of the organization's mission. Since the gathering was for a specific purpose, fundraising, all you had to do was be in harmony with that goal. Thus, the intended result of your talk was to get the crowd to be more generous.

On the other hand, the master of ceremonies might be more direct about what he wants from you. For example, "Joe, tell us why the opportunities in Singapore are depressing." In this case, you take that specific result — assuming you agree with it (why the opportunities in Singapore are depressing) — as your own. If you don't agree with the direct order, then talk about why the opportunities in Singapore are not depressing.

To summarize, your intended result is something specific you want to accomplish as a consequence of your talk. Anytime you hear a bad speech — one that meanders all over the map — you invariably know that the speaker has not nailed down what he or she wants to make happen.

2. Select a prop.

Why a prop? Using a prop is a terrific way to get your audience's attention. The prop points, which your audience helps you discover, become the basis for your persuasion points. The persuasion points allow you to develop ideas that truly move your audience in the direction of your intended result. The prop thus allows you to identify concepts that will be paralleled in your persuasion points. This parallelism helps your audience to more readily remember the content of your talk. Furthermore, since the prop is concrete and visual, it helps anchor your message in the audience's mind.

The best kind of prop to use is an *out-of-context* or *implausible* prop. An out-of-context prop enables you to get the audience's attention fast, arouse their curiosity, and involve them as you unfold your message. We have listed fifty-one props you might have at hand. Any one of them would serve should you unexpectedly be called upon to speak.

Possible Props from a Banquet Table

keys	paper money	coins
salt shaker	flowers	wallet
tie	shoe	glass of water
bottle	piece of paper	newspaper
pen	pencil	knife
fork	spoon	piece of chalk
light bulb	lamp	coffee carafe
cup of coffee	shoe lace	sock
belt	brassiere	earring
ring	watch	chair
telephone	briefcase	Danish
dessert	dirty dish	napkin
eyeglasses	comb	aspirins
antacids	condom	balloon
string	garter	stocking
mirror	lipstick	sneaker
mascara	necklace	picture off a wall

Incidentally, use good judgment in your selection of a prop. If you are speaking to a group of nuns, a condom probably would be a bad idea. If you choose a brassiere and your big boss is a woman, your clever idea might not seem so clever. Even though you seek an implausible prop, don't abandon common sense or good taste.

3. Select a subject of comparison.

The subject of comparison is always something or someone connected to the intended result. In this case, the flower arrangement is compared with the children who would benefit from larger donations to fight muscular dystrophy.

4. Get the audience involved.

The ASAP method not only structures your talk, but invites the audience to help you out. You simply build the discovery of your prop points and parallel persuasion points around questions to the audience. Through their responses, they provide you with the material for your talk. In fact, using this Socratic type of talk, speech preparation does not get any easier. What is more, the audience is involved, awake, and 100 percent attentive because you present them with a puzzle that arouses their curiosity and stimulates their thinking.

5. Use the ASAP shell.

The ASAP shell provides the key sentences, the key questions, and the framework for your talk. It only needs to be adapted on the spot to your specific speaking challenge. The shell is very simple and comes in four parts: the beginning, the bridge, the middle, and the ending. We provide examples from the earlier speech. Study the examples and parallel them for any speech.

I.   BEGINNING
      A.   *"Tonight, I want to talk about [your prop —*
             e.g., this arrangement of flowers]." (Three-

count pause) The introduction of a prop immediately captures the audience's attention.
B. *"In a minute I will tell you what it has to do
with [your intended result — e.g., fundraising]."*
This assures the audience that what you are
aiming for is relevant.
C. *"Now, focus on the [prop — e.g., the flowers]
and, if you would, answer some questions.
What are some of the positive and negative
aspects of [your prop — e.g., these flowers]?
What are its pluses and minuses? Some of its
significant features?"*

All you have to do is get the audience to respond. Listen to
them and, in your mind, select two or three points that apply to
your subject of comparison. If the audience is balky, suggest
some points yourself. However, if you approach them in a good-
hearted manner, they are usually quite responsive.

II. BRIDGE
Make a bridge between your prop (e.g., the flowers)
and your subject of comparison (e.g., the children).
The bridge starts with a question and is followed by
an answer. The answer is a statement of the analogy
between the prop and the subject of comparison (in
this case, the kids for whom the money is being
raised). Remember: the subject of comparison (the
kids) is always connected somehow to your intended
result.

Question: [your bridge] *"Now, you might be wondering,
'what does this [your prop — e.g., this flower arrangement] have
to do with [intended result — e.g., fundraising]?'"*

Answer: *"Just as these flowers* [prop] *are beautiful, fragile,
and need care* [three prop points], *these children* [subject of
comparison] *are beautiful, fragile, and need care* [three persuasion points]."

Notice that your answer is the statement of the analogy
between the prop and the subject of comparison.

The bridge is important because it connects the discussion of the prop points to the real points of your talk — your persuasion points. Notice the specific parallels between the two. The bridge also indicates what persuasion points you are going to talk about and in what order. The structure of your talk now becomes crystal clear.

III. MIDDLE (persuasion points developed through questions)

    A. *"In what sense does [the subject of comparison] possess the first characteristic suggested by the first prop point?* [e.g., "In what sense are these children beautiful?"). Wait for the audience's response.

    B. *"Just as the [prop] is [second point], in what sense does [the subject of comparison] have that characteristic?"* For example: "Just as these flowers are fragile, in what sense are these children fragile?" Wait for the response.

    C. *"Just as the [prop] is [third point], in what sense does [the subject of comparison] have that characteristic?"* For example: "Just as these flowers need care, in what sense do these children need care?" Wait for the response.

As a consequence of these questions, the audience is heavily involved. They are giving you the answers, helping you build your speech, and enjoying the event.

IV. ENDING (five sections)

    1. An announcement that you are about to end.

    2. A summary of three pains the audience will experience if they do not do what you want them to.

    3. A summary of three rewards the audience will reap when they indeed do what you want them to.

    4. A direct call to action.

    5. A final link between your prop and your subject.

THE ENDING FORMAT (WITH EXPLANATIONS)

1. Always start your ending with "In closing ..." or "In conclusion..." or "To summarize..." Starting this way lets the audience know that relief is in sight — you're almost through. Also, it scoops up their attention again for the most important part of your speech: the ending. The remainder of the first sentence of your ending is, "In conclusion, ladies and gentlemen, let me leave you with a few ideas."

2. The next part of the ending is where you drive home the points to sway them — your persuasion points. There are two major ways to persuade people to take action: either convince them they can avoid pain by following your advice or convince them they can reap some reward. We employ both. To make sure you have a strong, persuasive ending, remind them of three pains they will experience *if they do not do what you want them to,* and three rewards they will experience *when they do what you want them to.* Since this part of your speech will vary, depending on your intended result, it is best illustrated by going back to our previous example. First, the three pains:

"If this organization does not receive greater support from you,

These beautiful, fragile children will be stunted in their growth.

These beautiful, fragile children will experience painful rejection in their lives.

These beautiful, fragile children will die, far too early, from lack of care."

Notice the guilt trip you are inflicting on the audience. You intentionally want to make them feel uncomfortable; it will help you achieve your intended result. Besides, all your persuasion points have come from the audience's suggestions anyway, so they will accept them readily. Also, notice the anaphora "these beautiful, fragile children will ...," repeated three times. An anaphora is a wonderful figure of speech that helps you build your talk to an emotional crescendo. But your purpose is not just to inflict pain and guilt. You want to achieve your intended result. So, you use the other great motivator, reward, to show the audience how they can have peace of mind and satisfaction by doing a noble deed. Therefore, you follow with:

3. "On the other hand, when you open your hearts and pocketbooks, and add $100 to your plate ..." (this is your intended result, but notice that it is phrased in a way that is no longer conditional — we use *when* rather than the *if* associated with the pain of not doing it). Then you simply tell the audience the rewards they will reap when they do as you prescribe. For example, in our scenario:

"Your gift will provide them with a springboard to a cure.
Your gift will provide them with a springboard to proper medical care.
Your gift will provide them with a springboard to a fuller, happier life."

This way, you provide the audience not only with the pains they will experience if they are not generous, but with the rewards they will reap when they are generous. That is how you persuade people, by showing them how to avoid pain and reap rewards. Also, notice the second anaphora: "Your gift will provide them with a springboard to ..." By using this second anaphora, you establish a dramatic rhythm that makes your final call to action virtually irresistible.

4. Call to action — the next to last sentence.

Tell them what you want them to do. Be clear. Do not equivocate. Do not assume the audience automatically knows the right thing to do. Be like an effective salesperson: ask for the order.

"Ladies and gentlemen, open your wallets, pull out your credit cards, dust off your checkbooks, and let's make this spontaneous expression of your generosity a three-figured one."

5. Final link of prop to subject of comparison — the last sentence.

"And one final thought: As you look at the beautiful floral arrangements in front of you, (pause) think of our kids!"

Just as a play or story has a dénouement, so your speech has its outcome. This outcome has employed pauses, anaphoras, and dramatic builds to sway the audience, and a prop to anchor your talk in their minds. Since memory works through the suggestive power of association, your message will be associated with your prop and remembered long after the audience has forgotten most other speeches.

CONCLUSION

The ASAP method has countless applications: banquet speaking, sales conferences, parent–teacher meetings, fraternal club meetings, employee meetings, and so on. This same method can be used not only on the way to the podium, but even if you have more lead time. It is effective no matter when or where you use it. Simply imitate and adapt our model to suit your specific situation.

Mastering the ASAP method allows you to ask all the right questions. It makes impromptu speaking a lot of fun. The audience does all the hard work and has fun doing it. Use the ASAP shell and you need never fear a speaking opportunity again. You will always be prepared when you use ASAP. Test it out!

14

The Second-Fastest Way to Create a Memorable Speech

We feel certain that by now you are fully acquainted with the ASAP method. You know how to find a prop and how to use it to create persuasion points.

Occasions may arise, however, when you are reluctant to build your speech around an implausible prop or even a plausible prop. What occasions might those be?

1. "No one in my organization ever did it that way before."
   Since there is a profound pull in bureaucracies toward conformity and homogeneity, many workers and managers prefer not to stand out. And that, of course, is both the reward and the problem of giving an ASAP speech. If you use an implausible prop, you will stand out and your listeners will remember it. In many arenas, a low profile is the right ticket, and using an implausible prop would be a ticket to the wrong show.

2. "Others will say it's gimmicky."

Since a number of people in organizations are "other-directed," the fear that a colleague or (heaven forfend!) a boss might say that your speech was gimmicky (also read: theatrical, way out, unprofessional, weird, or different) is more than sufficient reason for them *not* to try an implausible prop.

3. "I'm not comfortable with trying something new."

When you use an implausible prop, you take a risk. It is something new, something different and unique — a slight step into the unknown. "I've always used the old tried-and-true methods of putting my speeches together and I've never had a complaint. Why should I bother to change? You say I'll do a great job if I use a prop, but what if I don't? I can't afford to bomb."

4. "I used a prop for my last four speeches. Maybe I'm in a rut and need something else — you know, more variety."

It is also possible that a lot of managers and professionals in your organization have recognized the effectiveness of an ASAP speech, and they are all bringing in implausible props (toads, broken chairs, diving boards, leaking coffee cups) to spice up their talks. Under these circumstances, you might feel you need a vacation from an implausible prop, no matter how effective it is.

Regardless of the reasons why you might balk at using a prop, you still have these problems facing you whenever you give a speech:

1. Limited time to put your speech together.
2. A need to make the speech memorable.
3. A need for something other than a prop to open your speech with a bang.

What can you do?

USE THE SECOND-FASTEST WAY TO CREATE A MEMORABLE SPEECH

As we have seen in the preceding pages, it takes no time at all to choose an implausible prop, a millisecond at most. It can be done without thought, without analysis or evaluation. And once you have selected your prop, you have a concrete object on which to focus your attention, speeding speech construction, freeing imagination, and creating associations that are lasting for both you and your audience. For the second-fastest way, we suggest you choose an implausible simile.

What Is an Implausible Simile?

First of all, let's make sure we know what a simile is. Then we will go over the difference between a plausible and an implausible one. We will also explore the advantages of using an implausible simile, and how to build a powerful speech around one.

A simile is a figure of speech that makes a comparison between two things that are essentially different but thought to be alike in one or more respects. The point of resemblance is expressed by *like, as,* or *as if.* A simile is used to highlight similarities, parallels, and likenesses beween two things.

A simile is different from a metaphor in that the comparison is explicit (for example, as American as apple pie, as bald as a billiard ball, as white as a sheet). Whereas a metaphor might talk about the whispering wind, a simile would say the sound of the wind is like a whisper. Although metaphors are more subtle, beautiful, and poetic, similes are clearer and less ambiguous. Similes are a better basis upon which to build a speech. Nothing, incidentally, prevents you from using metaphors throughout your speech. We advocate it. Metaphors give a speech verve and color that dry facts simply do not.

We mentioned that there are two kinds of similes: plausible and implausible. What is a plausible simile? It is one where the congruence, the fit, the similarity between the two things compared is smooth and readily apparent. In other words, it is easy to see; the image comes directly to mind. For example, these are plausible similes:

- She has a voice like an angel.
- The fire was like an erupting volcano.
- He drove like he was at the Indianapolis Speedway.
- They ate like hogs.
- His snoring sounded like he was sawing mahogany.
- He broke from the starting blocks as if he had been catapulted.

There is nothing wrong with using a plausible simile to build an ASAP speech (we will talk more about this later on), but the plain fact is: when it comes to constructing a memorable speech, a plausible simile is not as powerful as an implausible simile. Why? Because like an implausible prop, an implausible simile evokes curiosity and puzzlement in the listener. Its attention-getting power is greater. Remember: the hardest job for a speaker is to get the audience's attention. An implausible prop does that, and so can an implausible simile.

Let's take the plausible similes we mentioned above and convert them into implausible ones.

- She has a voice like a dollar bill.
- The fire was like ice water.
- He drove like linoleum.
- They ate like a hot tin roof.
- His snoring sounded like wet paint drying.
- He ran like the Goodyear blimp.

Notice what has happened? A plausible simile like "She has a voice like an angel" is so hackneyed, our ears barely hear it. But when her voice is compared not to an angel but to a dollar bill, your attention is captured immediately by the sheer incongruity of it. "I don't understand!" "What does he mean?" "Where's she going with this?" That is the reason we recommend using an implausible simile. Your audience will be puzzled. And when they are puzzled, they are awake, involved, and provoked. An implausible simile first grabs their attention, then arouses their expectations.

How Do You Use a Simile?

Basically you use a simile the same way you use a prop when you put together an ASAP speech. You must decide what your intended result will be. You must decide on your subject of comparison and make an audience analysis. Now all you need to do is plug into your memory bank and come up with something implausible that you can compare with your subject. After all, anything can be compared to anything.

It should not take but a few seconds to find an image, since most things in the universe (at least at first glance) are unlike your subject and seem far too dissimilar to make any sense. So it is quick and easy to come up with something implausible.

A Small Caveat About Using Implausible Similes

When you use an implausible simile to create an ASAP speech, choose an image that is wildly bizarre. Why? When you use a prop you have something real, concrete, and tangible to anchor your and the audience's attention. A prop is visible and can be pointed to throughout your speech. When you use a simile, you are employing something verbal, a figment of the imagination, an idea.

A simile is a word picture — something intangible, something you cannot pick up and hold in your hand. This has an advantage and a disadvantage. The advantage is that you are not limited by the size, weight, or portability of a simile. In fact, with a simile you are now without limits, and flights of even greater imagination are possible. The disadvantage is that it is easier for the focus of attention to drift (both yours and the audience's). That is why we cannot stress enough that if you decide on a simile, choose one that is vividly, wildly, bizarrely implausible — a word picture the audience will never forget.

Where Do I Go from Here?

Once you have an implausible simile in mind, the method is basically the same as building an ASAP speech around a prop. You come up with points just as you would with a prop, and those, in turn, generate persuasion points.

For example, had Joe Parent decided to use an implausible simile, he might have opened his speech this way: "Tonight I want to talk about the death of Kong. (Pause) In a minute, I will tell you what the death of Kong has to do with firing fifty-nine teachers." Joe's implausible simile is. "The death of Kong is like the firing of the fifty-nine teachers."

When Joe uses a simile like this, he brings his listeners to the foot of the Empire State Building and evokes a myriad of feelings about the tragic mistake of King Kong's death. Granted, Joe cannot literally hold King Kong up to view, as he could a prop like his shoe. But the word picture he paints of the death of King Kong conjures up a vivid image in the audience's imagination. And the implausibility of King Kong juxtaposed with the fifty-nine fired teachers grabs the audience's attention and causes them to wonder.

The advantage of an implausible simile is its lightness. It is easily transported to the podium and from there into the audience's imagination. Paradoxically, the disadvantage of an implausible simile is that imagination is not always equally distributed among people, any more than is intelligence or talent. Some people simply do not possess a bit o' the poet. They see only what is in front of them. Their sensitivity to word pictures has long been replaced by the exact delineations of a slide rule. The left side of their brains is overdeveloped at the expense of the right side (the side comfortable with feelings, images, and insight).

If you use a simile, therefore, you are stuck with the paradox. Implausible similes are bizarre and for that reason will break through to more tough-minded people than will plausible similes. But some minds may be turned off to any simile. And, unlike a tangible prop, you cannot use a simile to beat them over the head if they start to nod. Nevertheless, an implausible simile will captivate *most* of your audience.

THE ASAP SPEECH USING AN IMPLAUSIBLE SIMILE

You go through the same steps you would take if you were putting together the ASAP speech using a prop. You start at the end and define your intended result. "Why am I giving this speech? What change do I want the audience to make? What do I want to have happen?" You still need to go through an audience analysis asking the usual "who, what, when, where, why, and how long?" questions. Then you compare your image (prop) to your subject of comparison.

The Death of Kong Is Like Firing the Fifty-Nine Teachers.

Let's continue with Joe Parent. Joe wants to get the fifty-nine fired teachers rehired. In the original ongoing example, the prop was Joe's shoe. The subject of comparison was the fifty-nine teachers. Now, by choosing the image of the death of King Kong, Joe creates an implausible simile by comparing the image to the firing of the fifty-nine teachers — Kong's death is like the firing of the fifty-nine teachers. Joe chooses this comparison because it is implausible. It is not readily apparent to the audience what King Kong's death and the firing of fifty-nine teachers have in common. Granted, both events are tragic. But other than that, the similarities are fairly murky. It is an incongruous comparison and its shock value gives it power.

What next? Once again, just as you did with a prop, you fashion a Ben Franklin Mind Map listing the good and bad aspects of your implausible image (in Joe's case, the death of King Kong). Remember the process? A circle in the middle of the page with a vertical line in its center, pluses to the left and minuses to the right. See *Figure 14.1.*

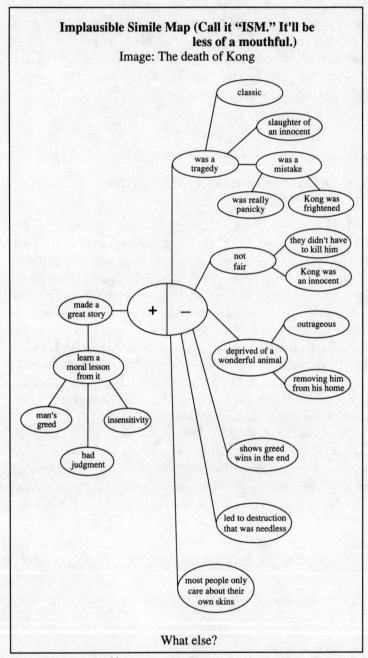

Figure 14.1: Ben Franklin Image Map Points

In the next step, you transfer your key simile points to the persuasion point map in order to jumpstart your analysis.

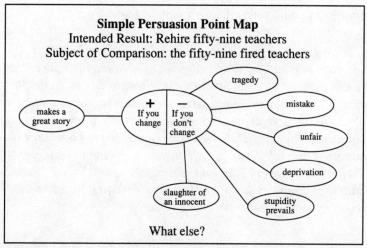

Figure 14.2: Simple Persuasion Point Map

We are not going to replow the whole field of mind mapping again. We just wanted to get you started so you could see that mapping a simile's image is exactly like mapping a prop.

Now let's move on to Joe Parent's example so we can show you what his speech would have looked like had he used the implausible simile of the death of Kong. We will comment along the way to remind you of the basic ASAP method.

SCENE

Joe Parent approaches the podium with his outline in hand. He places it on the podium, smiles and says:

"Ladies and gentlemen, tonight I want to talk about the death of Kong. (pause)

"In a minute I will explain what it has to do with rehiring our fifty-nine teachers.

"But right now, let's focus on the death of Kong."

(Notice that Joe uses the standard ASAP opening and he promises that his talk will be relevant to the subject.)

"I'm sure most of you have seen this classic of cinematic art. It's the story of what happens to a giant ape. At the opening of the movie, we see this huge innocent creature living an idyllic existence on a lush island somewhere in the Pacific. There's plenty to eat, and all his needs are met. But into the midst of this paradise comes the white man who has different plans for this oversized animal. These greedy men can see only dollar signs. They capture the ape, put him in a cage, and sail for the United States, planning to make millions by displaying him as a side show freak. They name him King Kong!

"These self-serving men bring Kong to New York, that mecca of kindness and understanding. They set up their show in a grand ballroom and invite the press. All New York throngs to see the monster. When the curtain goes up on opening night, the crowd roars and flashbulbs pop. Kong, who is chained to a stanchion at one end of the ballroom, becomes terrified by the clamor. With a mighty scream, he snaps his chains as if they were made of spaghetti and flees from the building.

"Instinctively, Kong feels that if he can get up someplace high, he will be safe. That's the way it works back in the jungle. So he climbs to the highest place in New York City — the top of the Empire State Building.

"But the planes come and strafe him with bullets. He loses his grasp and falls. He hits the concrete, but before he dies, he opens his hand to let his true love escape unharmed.

"This was a mistake. It should never have happened. This was the slaughter of an innocent — something that got completely out of hand. This was a tragedy. And this tragic story will live on and on to teach man the evil of greed and power."

(Joe uses this part of the speech to elaborate the points he draws from Kong's experience. Next is the *bridge* to his persuasion points.)

"Now, what does this poignant story have to do with our fifty-nine teachers?

"The death of Kong is like the firing of these fifty-nine teachers.

"Just as the death of King Kong was a mistake, the slaughter of an innocent, and a tragedy, firing these fifty-nine teachers is a mistake, the slaughter of innocents, and a tragedy."

(Now Joe moves into his persuasive argument, paralleling the simile's image points evoked by Kong's story. Each point is elaborated by explanation and examples — E & E.)

"Before the era of tight budgets and this magnet school nonsense, our schools here in Jefferson had an enviable reputation throughout not only the county but the state.

- *Our students scored very high on the CATs and SATs.*
- *Over eighty percent of the time, our students got into colleges of their first choice.*
- *We were far above the state average for producing students who go to college.*

"But our new superintendent, like the captors of King Kong, arrived here in Jefferson wild-eyed and self-serving, touting the extraordinary advantages of magnet schools. He thought he had something better! What a mistake! Why?

- *It ignores the classic three Rs.*
- *It replaces substance with nothing but form.*
- *It costs millions more than our town can afford.*

"And how have you, our school board, our local intelligentsia, how have you resolved the budget shortfall? You put your collective brains together and decided to fire fifty-nine teachers.

That's how you find the money to implement our magnet schools. I consider this a slaughter of the innocents — the innocents being both the teachers and the students:

"These wonderful teachers, whose dedication has already given our town its illustrious reputation;

These students who would be deprived of the excellent education they are now receiving.

I can predict which way the CATs and SATs will go.

I can predict that many of our students will be denied the college of their choice.

I can predict that fewer will decide to go to college.

"What a tragedy this is.

Our town's reputation for quality education will go.

Our dedicated professionals will leave us and go where they are appreciated.

Our students will learn that buzzwords are more important than the real thing."

(Joe has been developing his persuasion points with explanations and examples, paralleling the key simile points. Now he moves to the standard ASAP *ending:* announcement, three pains, three rewards, call to action, and final linkage.)

"In conclusion, let me leave you with a few thoughts.

If you do not rehire these fifty-nine teachers,
You are choosing to frustrate our children's futures.
You are choosing to decimate our distinguished teaching staff.
You are choosing to destroy our community's hard-earned reputation for educational excellence.

"On the other hand,
When *you rehire these fifty-nine teachers,*
You are voting yes to quality education in Jefferson.
You are voting yes to our children's future.
You are voting yes to our community's reputation."

(Notice the anaphoras "you are choosing" (repeated three times) and "you are voting" (repeated three times). Notice the use of *if* and *when*.

"Ladies and gentlemen of the school board, there is only one course of action: rehire these fifty-nine teachers!

"And one final thought. Let's not be responsible for Kong dying again."

Now let's summarize:

1. Beginning: standard, except instead of presenting a prop, you state the image of your simile — that's your opener
2. Simile points highlighted (the death of King Kong): mistake, slaughter of an innocent, tragedy.
3. Bridge question
4. Parallel persuasion points: mistake, slaughter of innocents, tragedy.
5. Closing — use of anaphora: three pains *if,* three rewards *when.*
6. Intended result (call to action): tell them what to do
7. Final linkage of subject to simile: teachers to Kong

POST SCRIPT ON PLAUSIBLE SIMILES

Even though we advocate using an implausible simile within the ASAP frame, you may still feel a little exposed if you use it. You may feel it's out of place for your particular speaking opportunity. If that is the case, then just as we suggested in Chapter 11 that you substitute a plausible for an implausible prop, we counsel you now to substitute a plausible simile. Let's see how Joe Parent would have dealt with this.

A Plausible Simile (in this case also an intended result)

"Please don't let our schools become like Richmond's schools." (This is an example of a city that tried magnet schools, and the experiment proved to be a gigantic failure.)

Joe still opens his talk in the standard ASAP way: "Tonight, ladies and gentlemen, I want to talk about Richmond, California. (pause) In a moment..." (and so on).

Joe then elaborates on Richmond's experience. He makes his bridge to the persuasion points exactly as he did before. His persuasion points parallel his simile points, and he develops them through explanation and examples (E & E). He employs the standard ASAP ending: the announcement of ending, the anaphoras used with pain and reward, the call to action, and the final linkage.

Thus, the ASAP shell can accommodate a plausible simile just as easily as an implausible simile, a plausible or implausible prop. Just keep in mind that the more you drift away from implausibility in your comparisons, the less memorable your speech will be, for both you and your audience. However, be assured that if you continue using the ASAP shell, your speeches will still be 500 percent better than anybody else's, no matter how plausible your openers become!

In the next chapter, we show you how to achieve even more variety in creating speeches by using the basic ASAP shell.

15

Other Ways to Create a Memorable Speech

The ASAP method provides you with a framework for speech construction that can incorporate many more traditional ways of building a speech while integrating the parts of the speech into a unified, coherent whole.

Most experts agree that how you open your speech is critical. Imagine a railroad engine at rest. It takes far more energy and effort to overcome the engine's inertia and get it in motion than it does to keep it in motion. Think of your audience as that engine. They are waiting for you, the engineer, to fire them up and get them rolling down the track. They expect it. That is what they are there for — to be moved. Your job is to electrify them, put steam in their boilers, get their wheels turning. If you fail at this, the ride is sure to be jerky and unproductive.

OPENING STRATEGIES

Some writers of speech books counsel you to open your speech with a joke. A joke breaks the ice, they say, it warms up the audience, establishes rapport, gets them in a good mood, and helps them to have positive feelings toward you. Once you have accomplished that, the rest is easy.

Others suggest a dramatic stunt as the best way to begin a speech — firing a gun, making pigeons fly out of your coat pocket, or tripping (like Chevy Chase) on the way to the podium. Stunts like these certainly do startle the audience and grab their attention.

Still others teach you to start with a story, a startling fact, a rhetorical question, a short poem, or, like a typical preacher, a quotation from the Bible or some other noted source. The problem with these ways is that they often have nothing to do with the content of the speech. They are simply icebreakers. The body of the speech is disconnected from the icebreaker and meanders all over the lot.

We contend, however, that any one of these openers is a valid alternative to using an implausible prop. Let us assume there comes a time, for whatever reason, when you decide against using a prop (plausible or implausible) or a simile (plausible or implausible) as your speech opener. You want something else, something different. But what? You know that regardless of the way you choose to open your speech, you are still left with the nagging questions "What else do I say?" and "Will what I say relate to my opener?"

The ASAP method, which is basically an argument by analogy, can effectively use any of the opening strategies mentioned above. After you decide on your intended result and do an audience analysis, you follow the exact same procedure as you would for a prop or a simile.

In *Figure 15.1* we show an outline that integrates the various openings with the ASAP shell. It helps answer "Will what I say relate to my opener?"

Outline Using Diverse Openers and the ASAP Shell

I.   What is my intended result?

II.   Audience analysis (Who, What, When, etc.)

III. What kind of opener will I use? (Joke, stunt,

startling fact, story, rhetorical question, short

poem, or quotation.)

IV.   What will I compare my opener to? (subject of comparison)

V.   Apply the ASAP shell

   A. Beginning

     1. Opener

     2. Comparison to subject

     3. Attributes flow from opener to become opener points

       a. explanation for each

       b. examples for each

   B. Bridge

     1. Questions the comparison

     2. The answer spells out the parallels between

opener points and persuasion points

   C. Middle (persuasion points developed through questions)

     1. Questions about similarity of opener points and

persuasion points

     2. Answer — persuasion points

       a. explanation for each

       b. examples for each

   D. Ending

     1. Announcement of close

     2. Three pains (*if* — anaphora three times)

     3. Three rewards (*when* — anaphora three times)

     4. Call to action

     5. Final linkage

Figure 15.1: Outline for Diverse Openers

As you can see from the outline, any opener you choose can be fully integrated into your speech. No longer will a joke be used just to warm up the audience. No longer will a stunt be used simply to get the audience's attention. No longer will any of your openers be disconnected from the rest of your speech. You can plug virtually any opener into the ASAP shell and come up with a memorable, coherent, and fully integrated speech. How? A joke (story, quote, or other device) spawns joke points. Joke points generate persuasion points. And when the persuasion points are dressed in an anaphora and attached to the standard ending of pain and reward, you have yourself an excellent speech.

This process holds true for any type of opener you choose (see *Figure 15.2*). When you use the ASAP shell, any opener is fertile ground from which the beginning and middle of your speech can grow.

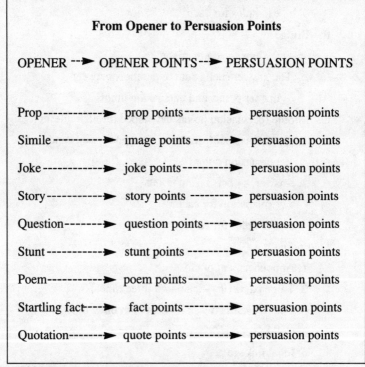

Figure 15.2: From Opener to Persuasion Points

Using this process of opener → opener points → persuasion points, you have answered the questions "What do I say?" and "Will what I say relate to my opener?" Once you go through this simple process, 90 percent of your speech construction is done.

(N.B. You must always decide first *what your intended result will be. Then you must ask "who, what, when, where, why, and how many" questions about your audience. These two steps must always be done first, no matter which opener you choose.)*

Developing Opener Content

Once you choose an opener, you must develop its content. You do that by employing the Ben Franklin Mind Maps. Here's what the process looks like when it is applied to any opener you might choose:

I.   Ben Franklin Mind Map of Your Opener
    A.   List the pluses and minuses of your opener
    B.   Develop opener points by explanation and examples
II. Transfer Opener Points to Persuasion Point Map (to jumpstart your imagination)
    A.   Develop points by explanation and examples — E & E
    B.   Create new persuasion points
III. Check Most-salient Persuasion Points and Number Them in Order of Importance
IV. Transfer any New Parallels from Persuasion Map Back to Opener Map
V.   Create a Linear Outline with Standard ASAP Components
    A.   Beginning — opener and opener points
    B.   Bridge
    C.   Middle — parallel persuasion points
    D.   Ending
        1.   "In conclusion…"
        2.   Anaphora (*if* — three pains)
        3.   Anaphora (*when* — three rewards)
        4.   Call to action
        5.   Final linkage

EXAMPLES OF OPENERS

Since Joe Parent has been such a stalwart trailblazer for us, let's continue to use him as an example. You have seen how he used a prop and a simile to develop his speeches. Now let's see how Joe deals with two other openers. We are not going to go through everything (the Ben Franklin Mind Maps, and so on) in detail. We will simply show you what Joe used as an opener and then give you the o tline of the speech Joe carried to the podium. (If you still ha\. questions about Mind Mapping and Persuasion Points, reread Chapters 4, 5, and 6 to freshen your memory.)

Remember, in addition to a prop and a simile, you can use any of the following as your opener:

- story
- joke
- startling fact(s)
- rhetorical question(s)
- quotation
- short poem
- stunt

We are going to use a story and a combination of startling facts and rhetorical questions as our two models for you to imitate. They will illustrate how to develop any other opener you might choose. The process is exactly the same.

A Story for Openers

A famous sage lived on a mountainside. People came from all over the world to learn from him. But two young men who lived in the village below were jealous of his fame. They hatched out a plan to make the wise man look foolish. The two young men figured if they could prove that he was not so wise, they would become famous themselves. They decided to present the wise man with a dilemma. And whichever horn of the dilemma the sage chose would be the wrong one.

This was their plan: One of them would put a little bird in his hand and hold it behind his back. Then he would ask the sage, "Is the bird in my hand alive or dead?" If the sage said it was dead, the young man would open his hand and let the bird fly away. If the sage said the bird was alive, the young man would crush it and show the sage the dead bird. No matter which way the sage answered, he would be wrong.

Delighted with their plan, the two young men climbed the mountain, approached the sage, and presented their question to him. "Is the bird in my hand alive or dead?" The sage paused and thought for a moment. Then he said, "The answer is in your hand."

Note the advantages of this story. It has drama, conflict, brevity, and an unexpected ending — all the ingredients to capture and hold the audience's attention.

Here's how Joe Parent outlined his speech using the wise man story as his opener.

JOE PARENT'S SPEECH

Outline: Rehiring Fifty-nine Teachers

I. BEGINNING
   A. "I want to tell you a story about…" — sage and dilemma
   B. "In a minute …" — connection with rehiring fifty-nine teachers
   C. "Right now…" — tell the story
   D. Bring out the story points
      1. The sage
         a. noted for wisdom (E & E)
         b. noted for service (E & E)
         c. noted for kindness (E & E)
      2. The two young men
         a. self-serving (E & E)
         b. cruel (E & E)
         c. devious (E & E)

        3. The bird
          a. innocent (E & E)
          b. powerless (E & E)
          c. pawn (E & E)

II.   BRIDGE
    A. Story — rehiring teachers?
    B. Why? — imperative to rehire them
    C. The story creates parallels
       1. The sage is like our school district
       2. The two young men are like our superintendent
       3. The bird is like our children and teachers

III. MIDDLE
    A. Persuasion points
       1. In what sense is our school district like the sage?
         a. noted for achievement of its graduates (E & E)
         b. noted for its outstanding dedicated teachers (E & E)
         c. noted for its creative curriculum (E & E)
       2. In what sense is the superintendent like the two young men?
         a. his agenda is self-serving (E & E)
         b. his arrogant imposition of magnet schools (E & E)
         c. his devious omission of magnet school failures elsewhere (E & E)
       3. In what sense are our children and teachers like the bird?
         a. they are truly the innocents (E & E)
         b. they have little power or influence (E & E)
         c. they are being used as pawns (E & E)

(N.B. This outline may seem a little lean to you. Just remember that the way opener points and persuasion points get developed

is through explanation and examples (E & E). The more you elaborate by using E & E, the more you flesh out your speech. If you are concerned about remembering at the podium, simply jot down the key word(s) of your example after each opener or persuasion point.)

IV.   ENDING ("In conclusion...")
    A.   Pain — *"If* you decide not to rehire the fifty-nine teachers" (anaphora three times)
        1.   "You are choosing to crush the reputation of our school district"
        2.   "You are choosing to be bulldozed by our superintendent and his slippery promises"
        3.   "You are choosing to frustrate our children's futures and disrupt the lives of our fine teachers"
    B.   Reward — "On the other hand, *when* you rehire these fifty-nine teachers" (anaphora three times)
        1.   "You will be voting 'yes' to our tradition of excellence,"
        2.   "You will be voting 'yes' to the triumph of common sense over self-serving,"
        3.   "You will be voting 'yes' to our children's future and our teacher's value to our community"
    C.   Call to action — "only one course of action that makes any sense..."
    D.   Final linkage — "do not crush the beautiful, innocent bird you hold in your hand."

You now have an additional model of Joe Parent's speech. This time we developed it from a story that has no apparent connection with the firing of fifty-nine teachers. Next we show another example in which Joe uses a combination of startling facts and rhetorical questions. Once again, we assume you understand the ASAP shell; therefore, we will just give you a truncated version of Joe's speech in outline form.

STARTLING FACTS–RHETORICAL QUESTION OPENER

I. BEGINNING
    A. Opener
        "Ladies and gentlemen, I want to talk to you
        tonight about parochial schools. (pause) You
        may be wondering what parochial schools have
        to do with the firing of our fifty-nine teachers.
        I'll tell you in just a moment. But first, some
        questions you might find interesting.

        • Do you know that parochial schools in the
          United States graduate more college-bound
          students than public schools?
        • Do you know their graduates have higher
          levels of career success than public school
          graduates?
        • Do you know that parochial school students
          have higher CAT and SAT scores than public
          school students?
        • Do you know that parochial schools have
          lower drop-out rates than public schools?
        • Do you know that parochial schools accom-
          plish all this with roughly half the money that
          public schools spend?"

*(Note that you have all the ingredients of the standard ASAP
opening. Now you continue with your fact–question points.)*

    B. Opener points
        1. Tremendous support for teachers
            a. in choice of curriculum
            b. in matters of discipline
            c. in classroom freedom
        2. Tradition of teaching responsibility
            a. no coddling
            b. no ignoring violations
            c. no burden of paper reports

3. Focus on the basics
   a. teach the three Rs
   b. believe in mastery learning
   c. drill, practice, and rote learning are okay

II. BRIDGE
   A. Question
      "What does this have to do with rehiring our fifty-nine teachers?"
   B. Answer
      "Everything. Because before our new superintendent dazzled us with extravagant plans for magnet schools (at equally extravagant costs), our Jefferson school system was quietly being not only one of the best public schools in the county, but one of the best in the state. It was the equal of — and even surpassed — the level of most parochial schools. It had many of the same attributes of parochial schools. But now, that's gone. Support for the teachers is gone. Student accountability is gone. The three Rs are gone."

III. MIDDLE
   A. "In what sense is support for teachers gone?"
      1. No say in curriculum — imposed from headquarters (E & E)
      2. In discipline — teacher assumed to be at fault (E & E)
      3. In classroom — constant criticism by supervisors (E & E)
   B. "In what sense is student accountability gone?"
      1. Feel-good-about-yourself is primary (E & E)
      2. Ten strikes and you are still not out (E & E)
      3. Teachers punished by paperwork (E & E)
   C. "In what sense has the focus on the basics shifted?"

   1. Down with three Rs, up with costly trivia
      (E & E)
   2. Mastery learning vs. familiarity (E & E)
   3. Learning by osmosis (E & E)
   D. "And what is in its place?"
   1. Magnet schools
   2. Exorbitant costs, supported by firing our
      59 teachers.
IV. ENDING — "Ladies and gentlemen, let me
   conclude..."
   A. Pain (*if* — anaphora three times)
   B. Reward (*when* — anaphora three times)
   C. Call to action
   D. Final linkage — "One final thought..."
   1. Tradition
   2. Basics
   3. Accountability

So now you have it. We have developed diverse outlines for
Joe Parent's speech that cover the use of an implausible prop, an
implausible simile, a story, and startling (facts–rhetorical)
questions.

It should be apparent by now that the ASAP model remains
the same, no matter which opener you choose: a stunt gives rise
to stunt points that in turn generate persuasion points; a joke
creates joke points that spawn persuasion points; a quotation,
quote points, and so on.

The ASAP approach gives you a simple method that has room
for lots of variety. If you are a little shy about using a prop, then
try some other opener. No matter which one you choose, the
ASAP shell and format will provide the fastest way to create a
memorable speech. ASAP is a method for all seasons.

APPENDIX A

The Right Questions to Ask

I.   What *result* do I intend to bring about by giving my talk?
1. *Why* am I giving this talk? *Why* is the audience there?
2. *Who* will be in the audience?
3. *What* position does the audience have about my subject?
4. *When* will my talk be given?
5. *Where* on the program am I?
6. *How* long should I talk?
   Now that I've considered these questions, do I need to revise my *intended result*?
II.   What (implausible) *prop* should I use?
1. What are the pluses and minuses associated with my prop? (Display on a Ben Franklin Prop Map)
2. What explanations and examples can I use to elaborate prop points? (Add to the Ben Franklin Prop Map)
III. What can I compare my prop with? (The subject of comparison, that is, something connected to the intended result)
IV.   What does my Ben Franklin Persuasion Map look like

after I transfer my prop points (without explanation and examples)?

V. With my focus on one persuasion point at a time, and with the subject of comparison and the intended result firmly in mind, what are the pains the audience will experience if they *do not* change the way I want? What are the rewards they will reap when they *do* change? (Display them on a Ben Franklin Persuasion Map)

VI. As I look at my expanded Ben Franklin Persuasion Map, what points enable me to present my strongest case? (Check them)

VII. In what order should I place my persuasion points? (Number them from the most to least important)

VIII. Taking my cue from the selection and order of the persuasion points, how do I select and order my prop points?

IX. What does a coherent outline of my prop points and persuasion points look like?

X. What does the *bridge* between my prop points and my persuasion points consist of?

XI. What are the key words of the ASAP shell relating to my *beginning* for this speech?
   1. Opening sentence?
   2. "In a moment..." sentence?

XII. What are the key words of the ASAP shell relating to my *ending* for this speech?
   1. "In conclusion..."
   2. Three pains, preceded by first anaphora — *if*
   3. Three rewards, preceded by second anaphora — *when*
   4. Call to action?
   5. Final link of prop to subject of comparison?

XIII. How does the final, cleaned-up, inclusive *outline* look?

XIV. How do I prepare for D-Day?
   1. Number of rehearsals?
   2. Relaxation exercises?
   3. Focus on whom?
   4. What will I visualize?
   5. How early will I arrive to stage the show?

Buona Fortuna! Break a leg!

APPENDIX B

A Fully Developed Speech Using the ASAP Method: "Honoring Twenty-five Years of Service"

First, we give you the scenario, then Ben Franklin Mind Maps for the prop points and persuasion points, followed by an outline of the speech, and finally the transcript of the speech that was actually delivered.

SCENARIO

The president of a company is asked to honor associates who have served the company for twenty-five years. His intended result is to have the associates and their spouses feel appreciated and honored. Following the ASAP method, he chooses his watch as a prop, from which he draws prop points that generate persuasion points.

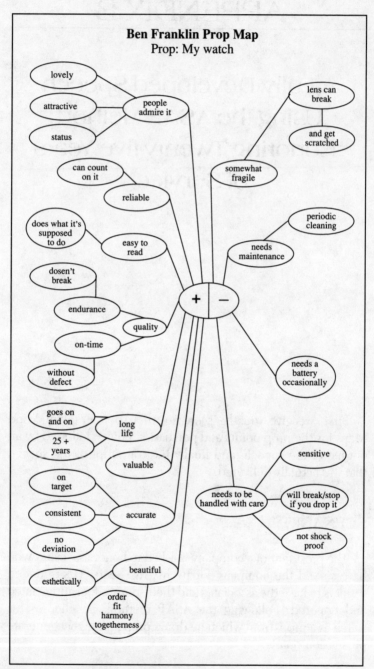

Figure App. B.1: Ben Franklin Prop Map

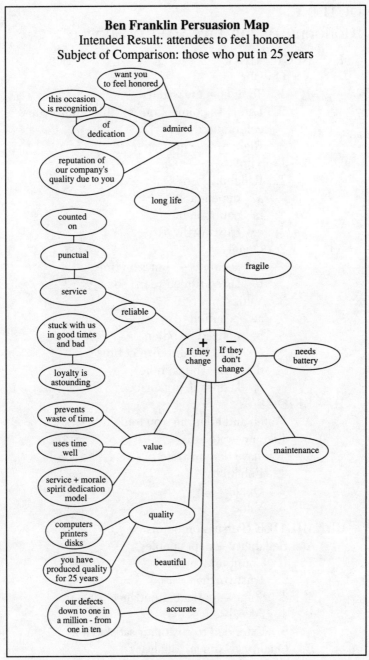

Figure App. B.2: Ben Franklin Persuasion Map

OUTLINE
"Honoring Twenty-Five Years of Service"

I.   BEGINNING
    A.   Opener
       1.   Tonight — my watch
       2.   Later — connection to this anniversary celebration
       3.   Right now — my watch
    B.   Prop points
       1.   Reliability?
          a.   dependable
          b.   count on it
          c.   trustworthy
       2.   Quality?
          a.   accurate — always on time
          b.   lasted fifteen years, so far
       3.   Value?
          a.   beautiful
          b.   noticed by others
          c.   gives me the correct time
          d.   keeps me on time
          e.   keeps me organized

II.   BRIDGE
    A.   Watch and honoring you tonight?
    B.   Like my watch...
    C.   You have demonstrated...
       1.   Reliability
       2.   Quality
       3.   Value

III.   MIDDLE (Persuasion points)
    A.   Reliability — dependable?
       1.   Count on
       2.   Trustworthy
       3.   Some — perfect attendance
       4.   Few absences
       5.   Extended to customer satisfaction
    B.   Quality — "you are quality"?
       1.   Work ethic

      2. Attitude — team spirit
      3. Service — few defects in work
      4. products in a museum
   C. Value — contributed added value: rippling effect?
      1. Company's reputation worldwide
      2. Value of our stock
      3. Created job security
      4. Enhanced community
      5. You have been a "model"
IV. ENDING ("In conclusion...")
   (Before watch presentation)
   A. Rewards (anaphora three times)
      1. "*If* all our associates followed your example, we would not be number three in our industry, but number one"
      2. "*If* all our associates followed your example, our presence in the global market would be pre-eminent"
      3. "*If* all our associates followed your example, our company's vision would be accomplished in double-quick time"
   B. Call to action (anaphora three times)
      1. "I want you to feel appreciated"
      2. "I want you to feel honored"
      3. "I want you to know that our company is in your debt"
   C. Final linkage
      1. Your watch and our esteem for you

(For this type of speech, it is not necessary to introduce any pain, any negatives, or discomfort. The whole experience should be positive and warm, a true celebration.)

SPEECH

Celebrating 25 Years

We have interspersed our commentary throughout the speech. Keep in mind: we recommend you do **not** write out your speech word for word, but rather speak from an outline made up of **key words** you wish to remember. We provide this example simply to show you how the speaker elaborated on the key words to create a smooth-flowing talk.

"Good evening, ladies and gentlemen, and welcome. (pause) Tonight I want to talk about my watch." (pause)

(Takes watch off wrist and holds it so all can see. Refers to watch often as the rest of the talk develops.)

"In a minute, I'll explain what it has to do with tonight's celebration. Right now, let's focus on my watch."

(Assures them of the watch's relevance.)

"This watch has three outstanding characteristics:
It is reliable.
It exudes quality.
It is valuable."

(The prop points are identified and the order in which they will be talked about is given.)

"In what sense is this watch reliable?"

(Each prop point is introduced as a question.)

"It is dependable. I can count on it. It doesn't break down — doesn't spend a lot of costly time being repaired. It's durable. It's always there, doing what it's supposed to do.

"In what sense does it exude quality? The case is made of gold and it has a jeweled Swiss movement. It is accurate — always gives me the correct time. And so far, it's lasted me fifteen years without showing signs of becoming old and tarnished.

"In what sense is it valuable? First of all, it's attractive. I get lots of compliments on it. It conserves my time, because I always know exactly how long to allocate to each of my responsibilities. It keeps me organized. It prevents me from wasting time."

(Up to now we have presented the prop points. Next is the bridge.)

"Now what does this watch have to do with honoring all of you who have given 25 years of service to our company? This watch is, in many respects, just like you. Just as this watch reflects reliability, quality, and value, each one of you here tonight celebrating your 25th anniversary with our company has demonstrated reliability, quality, and value."

(From the bridge, we move into the middle of the speech, giving explanations and examples for each persuasion point.)

"In what sense have you been reliable?"

(Each persuasion point is presented as a question.)

"For 25 years we have been able to count on you. Count on you to come to work. Count on you not simply to show up and breathe all day, but to contribute in a consistent, craftsmanlike manner. Some of you here tonight have had 25 years of perfect attendance —"

(Their names are called out. They rise and receive applause.)

"This is simply astounding dedication and loyalty. All of you here tonight have a record of very few absences. That is dependability! And it has been reflected time and time again in superlative customer satisfaction ratings.

"I said this watch exudes quality. In what sense do you exude quality? Well, first of all, you (pause) are (pause) quality! The work ethic you have displayed over 25 years is without parallel. Certain foreign groups have taken to bashing the American worker and have commented on his laziness and ignorance. You put the lie to that viewpoint. Why? Because the workmanship coming from your hands has actually been put into the Museum of Modern Art. The stream of continuous improvements that you have initiated and still initiate is a sign of dedication of the highest order. The climate of morale and good fellowship you have created here in our workplace has been emulated by countless companies. No matter how you spell it, ladies and gentlemen — that is quality!

"I mentioned this watch has value. In what sense have you added value? First of all, the reputation of our company is acknowledged worldwide. In the recent Fortune Survey of Companies' Reputations, we were listed as number one in our industry. This is not just a blip on the curve. We have been in the top three for five years straight.

"Secondly, you have added value to our company's value — to our stock. In 25 years it has gone from $7 per share to $87. I hope you folks were a little smarter than I and bought it when it was low.

"Further, your work has ensured job security for all of us here. We have never had a layoff — nor do we plan one. Why? The product quality and reputation coming from your hands has never flagged. You are our best insurance against hard times.

"Another value that you have contributed is your presence in our community. The town we live in has been enriched by your participation in civic affairs.

"And lastly, perhaps the pre-eminent value you have contributed is your example. You are the models for the young workers coming up. Your example demonstrates to them in a real way the right attitudes, the exquisite craftsmanship, your legendary customer service, and your never-ending commitment to improvement. No amount of preaching these values by me will ever have the effect that your example gives. And for this we thank you.

"In conclusion, tonight it is my pleasure to present each of you with this exquisite Movado watch as a small token of our appreciation and a constant symbol of what you have done for our company.

"And I want you to know:

"*If* all of our associates followed your example, we would not be number three in our industry, but number one.

"*If* all our associates followed your example, our presence in the global market would be pre-eminent.

"*If* all our associates followed your example, our company's vision would be accomplished in double-quick time.

"Ladies and gentlemen, tonight I want you to feel appreciated. I want you to feel honored. And I want you to know that our company is in your debt.

"One last thought: each time you look at your Movado, (pause) be reminded of the esteem with which we hold you."

APPENDIX C

Speech with Podium Notes:
"10 Percent, with Quality"

(First, we give you the scenario, then Ben Franklin Mind Maps for the prop points and the persuasion points. Finally, we present an outline of the speech.)

SCENARIO

A plant manager receives notice from his boss that within the next year his operation must cut costs by 10 percent across the board. This must be accomplished without reducing the quality level in the manufacturing and shipping process.

The plant manager decides to speak to all his employees. He feels that if they fully understand *why* it is essential to do this, they will indeed carry it through.

He reads in the newspaper about an accident on the turnpike the night before. Four passengers were seriously injured when their car crashed into a guard rail. Police attribute the accident to a new tire that blew out.

The plant manager decides to use a blown-out tire as his prop. He will draw parallels between what happened in the accident and what could happen if his employees do not cut costs by 10 percent and still maintain quality.

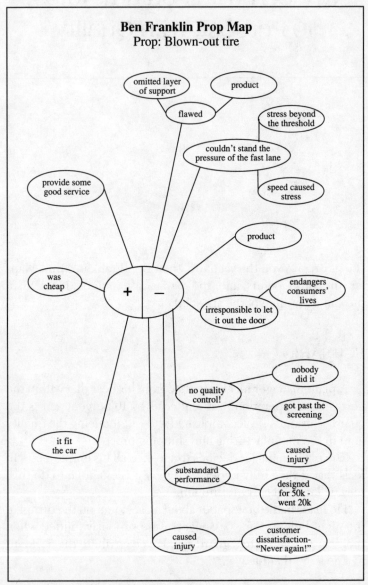

Figure App. C.1: Ben Franklin Prop Map

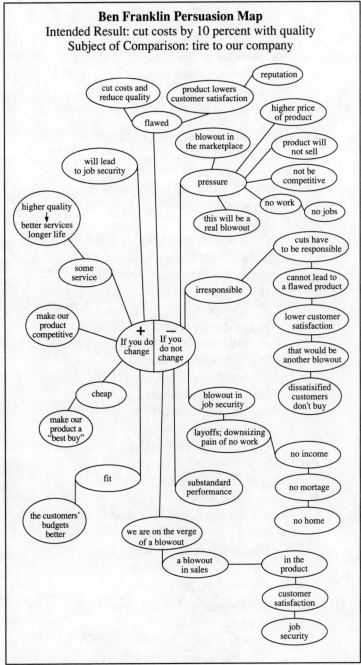

Figure App. C.2: Ben Franklin Persuasion Map

OUTLINE

Intended Result: motivate workers to cut costs by 10 percent
                 while maintaining quality
Prop: blown-out tire
Subject of Comparison: blown-out tire to our company

- I. BEGINNING (Opener and Prop Points)
    - A. Tonight — this tire
    - B. Later — connection to cutting costs
    - C. Right now — this tire (story about it)
    - D. Prop points
        1. Inferior product?
            - a. flawed construction (E&E)
            - b. pressure threshold low (E&E)
            - c. no quality control (E&E)
        2. Injury to customer?
            - a. four people hospitalized (E&E)
            - b. customer satisfaction (E&E)
            - c. even greater catastrophies (E&E)
        3. Injury to the company?
            - a. reputation evaporates (E&E)
            - b. tires get recalled (E&E)
            - c. no sales, no work, no jobs (E&E)
            - d. stock falls (E&E)
            - e. everyone loses (E&E)
- II. BRIDGE
    - A. Tire and our cutting costs?
    - B. Just as this tire blew out...
    - C. We will experience blowouts on three fronts if
      we do not cut costs and still maintain quality
        1. Blowouts in our product
        2. Blowouts in our sales
        3. Blowouts in our job security
- III. MIDDLE (Persuasion Points)
    - A. Blowout in our product?
        1. Run the risk of compromise (E&E)
        2. Cut the wrong corners (E&E)
        3. Doesn't meet quality specifications (E&E)

    4. Warranty costs will rise (E&E)

    5. Still have pressure to ship junk (E&E)

  B. Blowout in sales to our customers?

    1. High cost (E&E)

    2. Defective product (E&E)

    3. Lower satisfaction (E&E)

    4. Fewer sales lead to another blowout (E&E)

  C. Blowout in job security?

    1. No sales — no work (E&E)

    2. No work — fewer jobs (E&E)

    3. Fewer jobs mean layoffs (E&E)

    4. No income (E&E)

    5. No mortgage payments — no home (E&E)

IV. ENDING ("In conclusion...")

  A. Pain — "*If* you do not cut costs by 10 percent while maintaining quality...

    1. "we will have a blowout in the marketplace,

    2. "we will have a blowout with our customers,

    3. "we will have a blowout in our personal lives."

  B. Rewards — "On the other hand, *when* you do achieve a 10 percent reduction in costs while maintaining quality...

    1. "you can confidently get in the fast lane to increased sales,

    2. "you can confidently get in the fast lane to greater customer satisfaction,

    3. "you can confidently get in the fast lane to a future secured by a quality product."

  C. Call to action — "Only one course of action to take...10 percent, with quality."

  D. Final linkage — "The next time you look at the tires on your car, remember 10 percent, with quality."

Notice all the E&Es we have listed in this outline. The use of **explanations** and **examples** makes your speech flexible. On any given prop or persuasion point, your explanation and examples can be elaborate or brief, depending on how long you wish to talk or how deeply you wish to delve into your subject. Sometimes it is unnecessary to use E&Es, especially when you make a point that is self-evident. If you are worried about remembering all of your explanations and examples, most of them will come to mind once you see the key words on the outline of your prop and persuasion points. However, if it gives you greater comfort, include key words for any E&E that you are worried about.

There may be times when your speech requires graphs, tables, charts, or pictures. The E&E is where you introduce all supportive visual aids (e.g., slides, overheads, or handouts). However, we urge you to keep the lights on for your beginning and your ending and as much of the middle as you possibly can. If you use visual aids, remember to always talk to the audience, not to the slides. Your prop is still the best and most effective visual aid you will ever use.

APPENDIX D

Rules for Creating a Forgettable Speech

There are many ways to create and deliver a forgettable speech. We thought it might be useful to list a few of them, just on the off chance that some reader might want to consider them.

1. Do not prepare. Wing it!
2. Never rehearse.
3. Forget about who will be in the audience.
4. Stay unclear about how you want the audience to change.
5. Have a couple of martinis in advance to warm up your larynx.
6. Start your talk with an off-color joke.
7. Drape yourself casually over the podium.
8. Insult the audience if they look puzzled.
9. Use a lot of salty language.
10. Refer to particular groups in this way: the girls (or gals), the Japs, the colored (or worse), old geezers, Mafiosi, Injuns, homos, and so on.

11. Smoke while you speak, or chew gum and drink coffee.
12. Use "you people" a lot, and poke your finger at them.
13. Load up your speech with a lot of technical jargon. Punctuate each point with "You know?" or "Okay?"
14. Speak as long as you can. Think "Castro!"
15. Go into infinite (*ad nauseam*) detail.
16. Use hundreds of slides or overheads, and break it up midway through with a picture of a naked woman or baboons mating.
17. If you actually do prepare, read the whole speech and never look up.
18. Make sure you never look the audience in the eye.
19. Use graphs and figures loaded with information. Make the print very small. Never point out where the audience should look. Tell them the facts speak for themselves.
20. Follow these dress codes. For men: unbutton your jacket, loosen your tie, make sure your fly is unzipped, and have lots of pens and pencils in your plastic pocket protector. For women: show a lot of skin and wear all the jangling jewelry you own.
21. Use examples that have nothing to do with your persuasion points.
22. Mumble a lot and stand behind the podium with the microphone at nose level so the audience can neither see nor understand you.
23. Jiggle your car keys in your pocket throughout your talk. Loose change is even better.
24. When you end your speech say, "That's it!" or "Any questions?" Or perhaps just belch.
25. Never use the ASAP method to create a memorable speech.

If you follow these rules dutifully, you will indeed deliver a forgettable speech. Our final suggestion: After you speak, do not pause but go immediately to the nearest bar and order an anesthetic to blot out the experience.

ABOUT THE AUTHORS
William Mooney

Bill is a two-time Emmy Award nominee and a 30-year veteran of the acting and directing professions. He has served G.E., Citibank, General Motors, U.S. Steel, Chase Manhattan, and many others as corporate spokesman for their television campaigns. IBM, American Express, General Foods, W.R. Grace, Pitney Bowes, DuPont, and Bulova, among others, have featured Bill in their corporate films. He wrote and produced the audio training tape *Money in Motion,* as a joint project for AT&T and The Ayco Corporation. He is the coauthor of *Banjo Reb and the Blue Ghost,* a Civil War play that tours yearly throughout America. But Bill is most familiar to TV audiences for his long-running role on ABC's *All My Children.* Filmgoers have seen him in *Second Sight, Network, A Flash of Green, C.A.T. Squad, The Next Man,* and *Beer.* On Broadway, he has appeared in *A Man For All Seasons, Lolita, The Brownsville Raid,* and others. For over a decade he toured his one-man show, *Half Horse, Half Alligator,* worldwide. It was recorded by RCA Victor and filmed by CBS. He has appeared on *The Today Show, The Tonight Show,* and *The Mike Douglas Show.*

Donald J. Noone, Ph.D.

Don founded his own company in 1974 and over the years has become widely known for outstanding work in the area of management and personnel development. Don has a doctor of philosophy in sociology from Rutgers University and his areas of special interest are stress management, creativity, organizational development, and public speaking. He was formerly a research associate at Cornell University Medical College and the Institute of Management and Labor Relations of Rutgers, and has taught at Rutgers and Hunter College of the City University of New York. He is the author of two books: *Teachers vs. the School Board* and *Score — Systematic Comprehensive Orientation to Results* and *Excellence,* a management by objectives planning program. Don has a long list of satisfied clients that looks like a "who's who of American business," including AT&T, Bell Labs, Chubb and Son, Exxon, General Electric, Johnson and Johnson, Lockheed, The Knoll Group, Prudential, Westinghouse, and hundreds of other business, educational, governmental, and nonprofit organizations.